職人という生き方

The Way of Life of Craftsmen

工匠的生活方式

江戸切子

Edo Kiriko

江戶雕花玻璃

もくじ Contents 目次

親子代々 Parent and Child, Generation after Generation
父子代代傳承
小林淑郎さん Yoshiro Kobayashi 小林淑郎先生 11

江戸切子の歴史 History of Edo Kiriko
江戸雕花玻璃的歴史 23

町工場に勤める Working in a Small Factory
在町工廠工作
株式会社 清水硝子 Shimizu Glass Corporation 清水玻璃股份有限公司 31

弟子入り、独立
Apprenticeship and Independence
拝師入門、獨立開業

江戸切子のつくり方 43
The Way of Making Edo Kiriko
江戸雕花玻璃的製作方法

江戸切子の文様 61
Designs of Edo Kiriko
江戸雕花玻璃的紋飾

高野秀徳さん 51
Hidenori Takano
高野秀徳先生

切子職人への道 65
The Path to Becoming a Kiriko Craftsman
成為雕花玻璃工匠的路程

見るなら・買うなら 70
If You Want to See / If You Want to Buy
觀摩・選購

はじめに

前言 In-roduction

日々の暮らしの中で、職人の仕事を見る機会が少なくなりました。ものづくり大国といわれる日本では、その根底を支える職人のなり手が不足し、その技の継承は危ぶまれています。

難しいことをさも簡単そうにやってみせる職人の手技。その仕事を間近に見る機会があれば、今日よりも明日、もっといいものをつくり出してやろうとする職人の心意気。その仕事を間近に見る機会があれば、今日よりも明日、もっといいものをつくり出するのではないだろうか。インターネットサイト「ニッポンのワザドットコム」は、職人がつくり出すものの魅力、職人という人間からあふれてくる魅力を発信することで、もっと多くの若者たちに職人を志して欲しいという願いではじめたものです。サイトのオープンから一年以上経るなかで、たくさんの職人さんたちと出会い、お話をうかがってきました。その内容は"編集記事"として順次サイトに掲載し多くの人に読んでいただくこともできかないました。

この本は、インターネットをご覧にならない方、あるいは情報は手に取ってじっくり読みたいという方に向けて、ニッポンのワザドットコム編集部がこれまで発信してきた情報を一冊にまとめたものです。また出版にあたり、日本の職人を取り巻く現状を海の向こうの人々にも知っていただこうと、英訳と中国語訳も新たに付け加えました。これまで以上に多くの方に読んでいただくことを、切に願っております。

最後に出版にあたり、多大なご協力をいただいた東京カットグラス工業協同組合のみなさまに、この場をおかりしてお礼申し上げます。

2011年7月　ニッポンのワザドットコム編集部
http://www.nipponnowaza.com

In everyday life, opportunities to see the work of craftsmen are becoming fewer and fewer. In Japan, a country which is called a manufacturing powerhouse, there is a lack of people willing to become craftsmen to support this foundation. This means that the continuance of these techniques is under threat.

The craft of a craftsman is to make something that is difficult look extremely easy. The spirit of craftsmen is to try and make tomorrow's work even better than what they produced today. If you have the chance to see up-close this kind of work, then we feel that this will help to reduce the current shortage of craftsmen. The Internet site nipponnowaza.com was started with the desire to see many more young people aspire to become craftsmen by showcasing the appeal of pieces produced by craftsmen and the overflowing attraction coming from those people called craftsmen. In the over one year that has passed since the launch of the site, we have met a great many craftsmen and had the opportunity to speak to them. The substance of these meetings has been serialized on the site as Editorial Articles and many people have had the chance to read them. This book is the result of the efforts by the nipponnowaza.com editorial staff to collect together into one volume the information which has previously been made available on our website.

This book is aimed at those who are unable to view the website and also those that would like to have the chance to actually hold the information in their hands and read it at leisure. Furthermore, English and Chinese translations have been added when publishing this book so that people overseas can also understand the current situation that surrounds Japanese craftsmen. It is our sincere hope that more people than ever before will get to read this.

Finally, we would like to take this opportunity to express our gratitude to everyone at Tokyo Cut Glass Industry Cooperative for their tremendous cooperation when publishing this book.

nipponnowaza.com Editorial Department, July 2011
http://www.nipponnowaza.com

在日常生活中，見識工匠工作的機會變少了。在被譽為工藝大國的日本，支撐其根基的工匠新手不足，令人擔憂技藝的傳承。

專業工匠的手藝能讓工作化繁為簡。明日更勝今日，希望能創造出更好的作品，這即是工匠精神的展現。若能夠近距離地觀摩工匠作業的話，那麼現在工匠不足的現象是否就能稍稍減緩呢？網站「日本的技藝.COM」期待能把工匠們作品的魅力，以及工匠這項職業所洋溢的魅力散發出去，進而讓更多年輕人願意投入工匠這項職業。在網站開設後的一年多裡，我們先後與多位工匠邂逅並得以參觀採訪。並將那些內容逐篇刊載於網站的「編輯記事」中，期望更多人可以閱覽參考。

本書是獻給無法閱覽網頁的朋友看的，或是針對想要細細品味文字的朋友，由日本的技藝.COM編輯部將目前為止所刊載過的內容集結成冊。另外藉由出版的機會，想讓海外的人們也能知曉有關日本工匠技藝的現狀，所以也新增了英文與中文翻譯。我們殷切期盼更多人可以閱讀這本書。

最後，這次出版承蒙東京雕花玻璃工業同業工會諸位先進的大力協助，謹在此致上最誠摯的謝意。

2011年7月　日本的技藝.COM編輯部
http://www.nipponnowaza.com

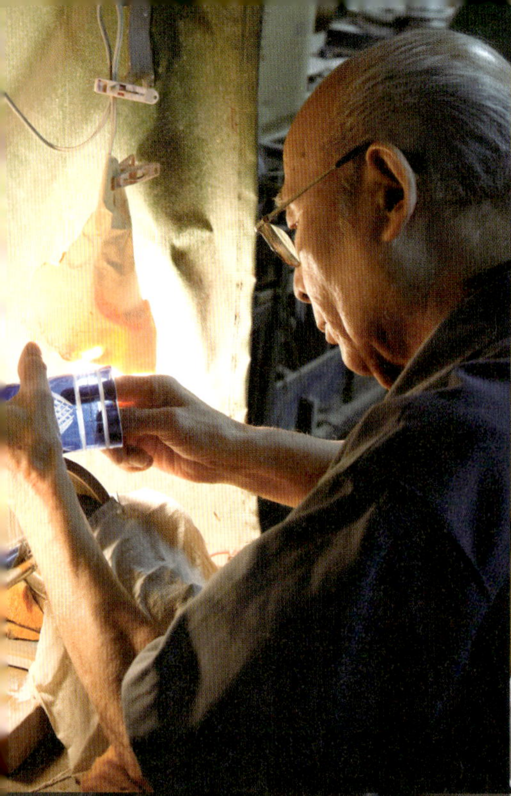
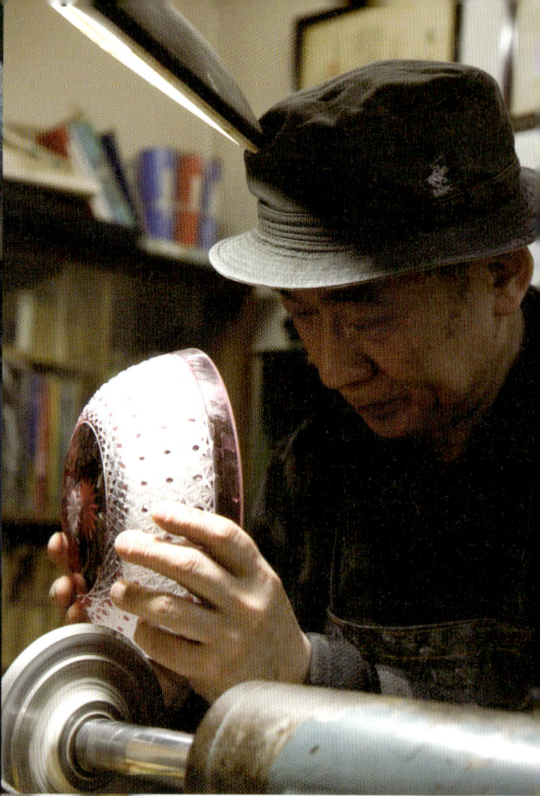
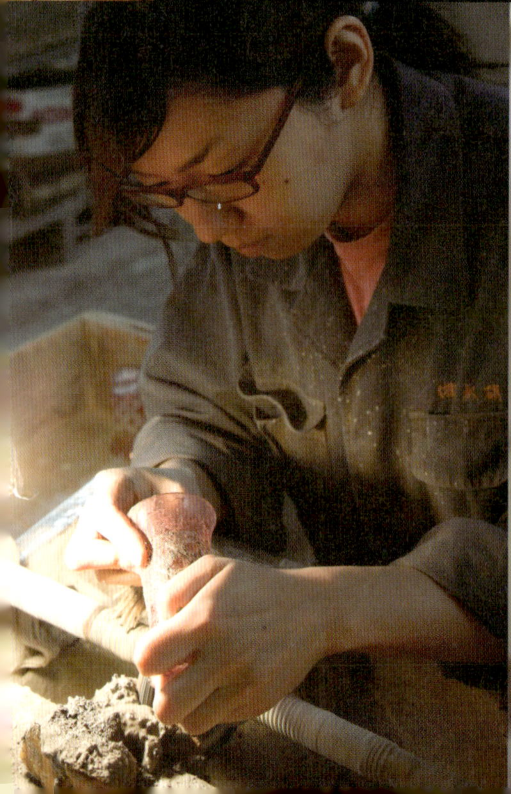
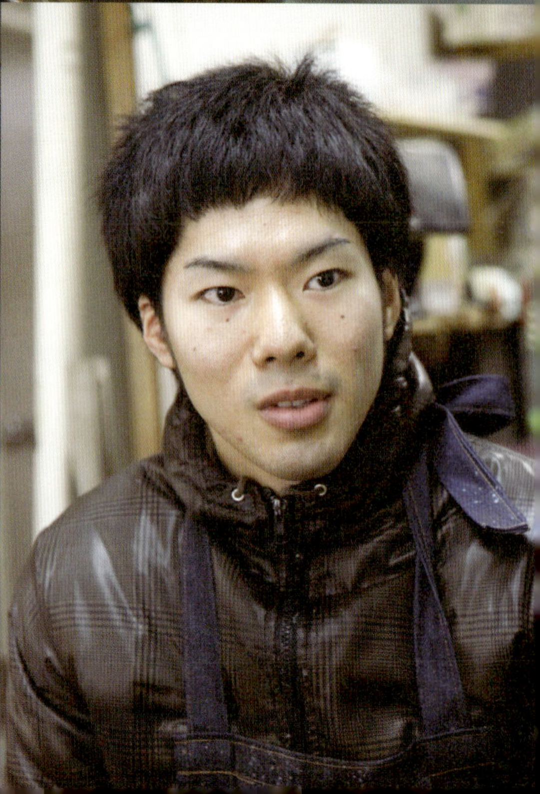

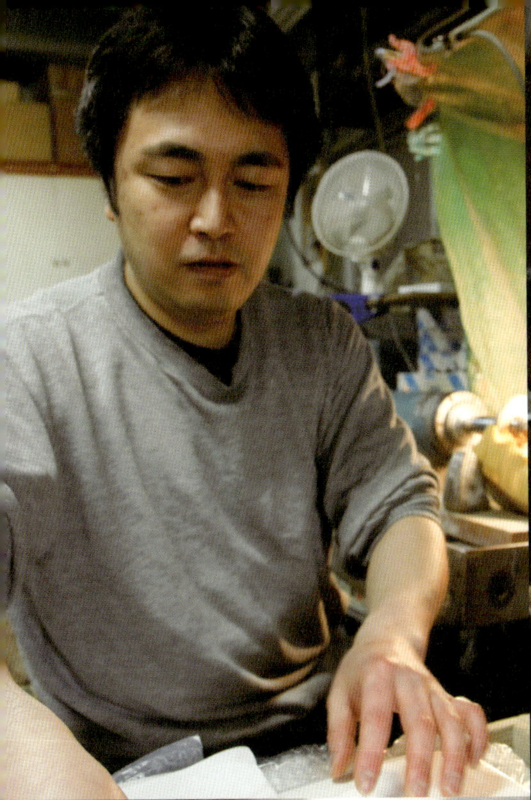
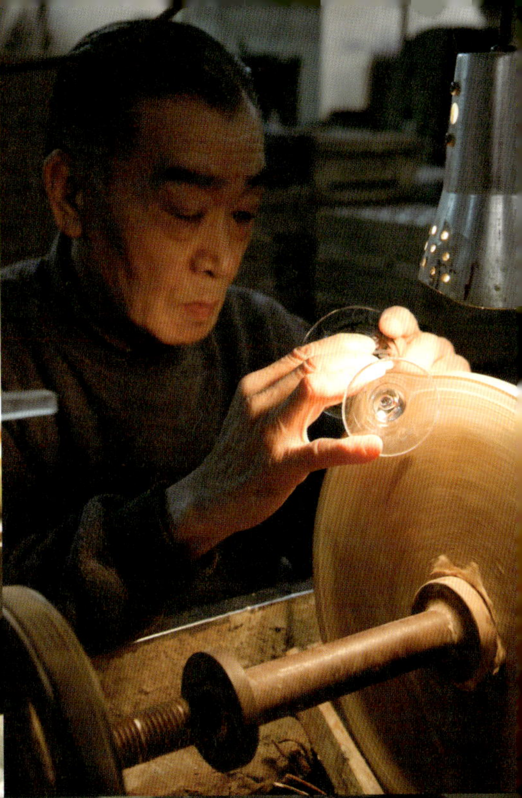
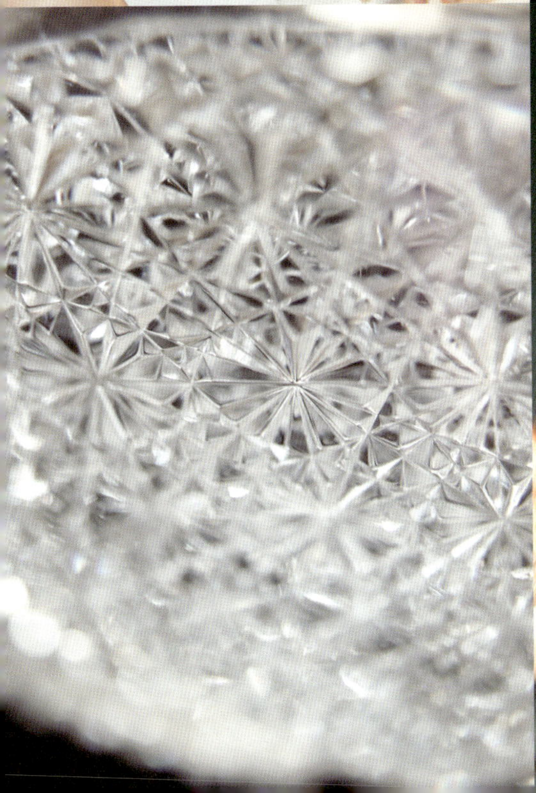
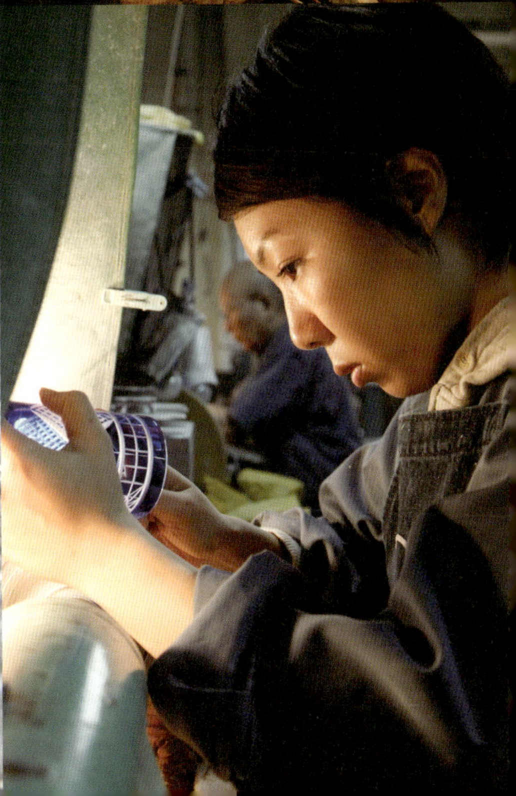

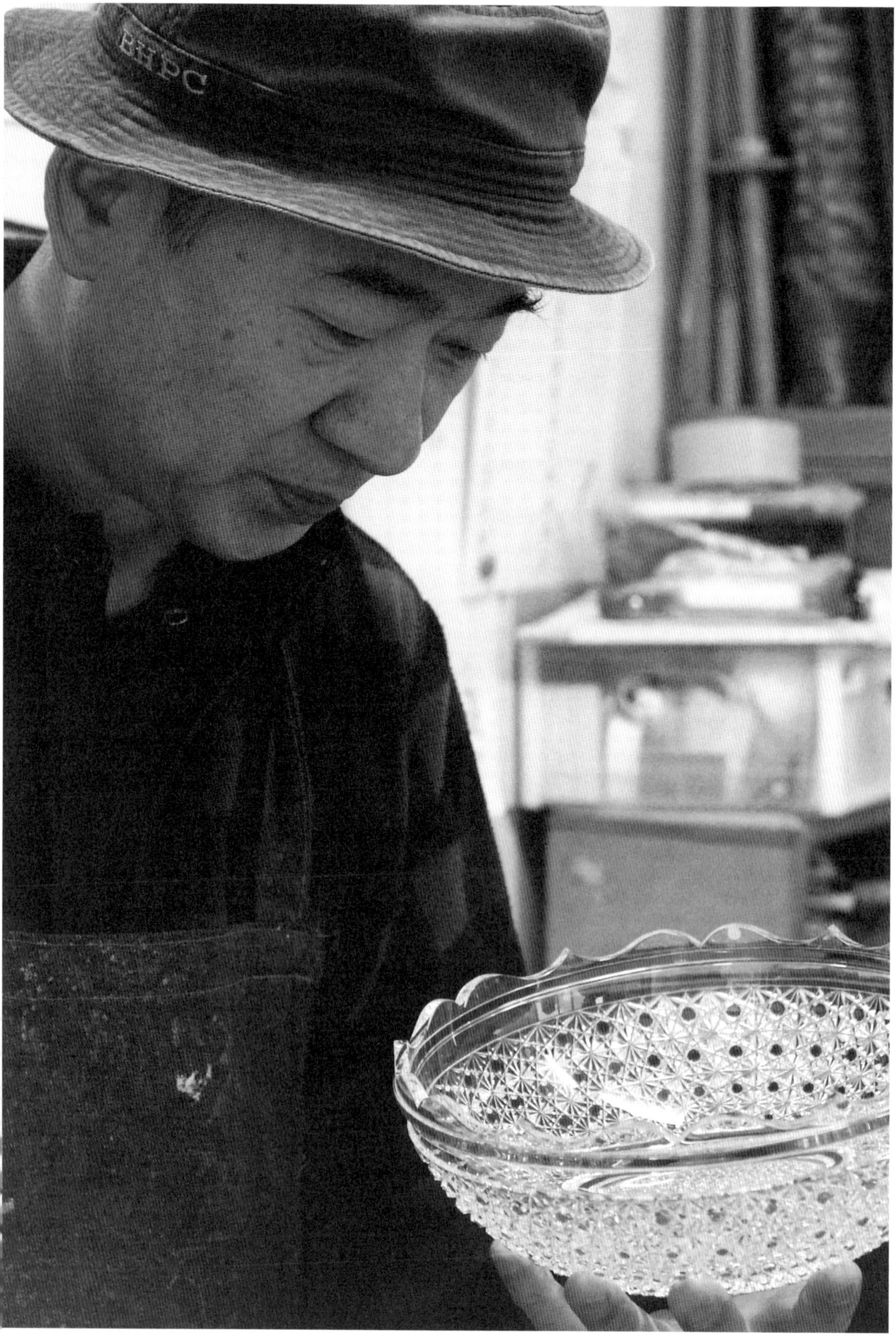
BHPC

親子代々

父子代代傳承

Parent and Child, Generation after Generation

小林淑郎さん
Yoshiro Kobayashi
小林淑郎先生

精緻な模様が刻まれる小林淑郎さんの江戸切子は、まさに芸術品。
国の伝統工芸士として活躍する小林さんは、お父様も「現代の名工」に選ばれた匠の腕を持つ江戸切子職人。小林家は親子三代にわたり、江戸切子のワザを継承していることになります。
そんな小林さんが、江戸切子職人になる意志を固めたのは、高校二年生の時だったそうです。
そしていま、息子の昂平さんが四代目となる意志を固めて修行中。代々、親子を魅了してきた江戸切子の世界についてうかがってきました。

The Edo Kiriko of Yoshiro Kobayashi, with his intricate patterns, is truly a work of art. Mr. Kobayashi plays an active role as a traditional craftsman of Japan. His father is also an Edo Kiriko craftsman with a talent that has seen him selected as a Contemporary Master Craftsman (an award from the Ministry of Health, Welfare and Labour to skilled craftsmen). The techniques of Edo Kiriko have been passed down through three generations of the Kobayashi family. Set against this environment, it was when Mr. Kobayashi was in the second grade of high school that his determination to become an Edo Kiriko craftsman hardened. Currently, his son Kouhei has developed the determination to become the fourth generation of Kiriko craftsman in his family and he is currently learning the trade. Generation after generation, have embarked upon the world of Edo Kiriko that attracts both parent and child.

小林淑郎先生製作的江戶雕花玻璃，細雕的精緻圖樣，簡直就是藝術品。小林先生是國家認定的傳統工藝士，他父親也是榮獲「現代名匠」認定的江戶雕花玻璃工匠。小林一家父子三代，持續傳承著江戶雕花玻璃的技藝。據說，小林先生立志成為江戶雕花玻璃，其關鍵是在高中二年級時。接著，現在其子昂平也堅定信念致力學藝，以期待成為第四代繼承人。現在就讓我們進入江戶雕花玻璃的世界，一同來窺探今這代代父子著迷的魅力吧。

プロフィール／東京都江東区生まれ。明治大学卒業後、父英夫氏に師事。1981年日本伝統工芸新作展入選。1983年第30回日本伝統工芸展奨励賞受賞、など受賞多数。2005年経済産業大臣指定伝統的工芸品「江戸切子」伝統工芸士に認定。2009年江東区無形文化財指定。東京カットグラス工業協同組合（江戸切子協同組合）元理事長。

個人簡介／出生於東京都江東區。明治大學畢業後跟父親（英夫先生）學藝。1981年入選日本傳統工藝新作展。1983年獲得第30屆日本傳統工藝展鼓勵獎等多項殊榮。2005年，榮獲經濟產業大臣認定的「江戶雕花玻璃」的傳統工藝士。2009年更被指定為江東區無形文化財。曾經擔任過東京雕花玻璃工業同業工會理事長。

Profile: Born in Koutou-ku, Tokyo. After graduating from Meiji University, Mr. Kobayashi took up study under his father, Hideo. In 1981, he won a prize in the Japan Traditional Crafts New Work Exhibition. Mr. Kobayashi has won numerous awards, including the 30th Japan Traditional Crafts Exhibition Honorable Mention Award in 1983. In 2005, he was certified as an Edo Kiriko traditional craftsman by the Minister of Economy, Trade and Industry who designates these traditional crafts. In 2009, he was designated an intangible cultural asset by the local government of Koutou-ku. He is the former Board Chairman of the Tokyo Cut Glass Industry Cooperative (Edo Kiriko Cooperation Association).

小林淑郎さんは国の伝統工芸士。
お父様である二代目の英夫さんは「現代の名工」に選ばれています。

Mr. Kobayashi is a traditional craftsman of Japan.
His father Hideo is a second-generation Edo Kiriko craftsman and has been selected as a Contemporary Master Craftsman.

小林先生為國家傳統工藝士。
父親英夫先生是創業後的第二代,曾被選為「現代名匠」。

素材の魅力を存分に引き出し、輝かせる江戸切子職人のワザ

　六月の梅雨が終わればもう夏。暑い夏にさわやかさをもたらしてくれるのが、ガラス細工です。今回はガラスの中でも江戸切子の職人さんたちを取材しました。最初におうかがいしたのは江戸切子の組合である東京カットグラス工業協同組合の理事長をつとめる小林淑郎さんです。小林さんは祖父の代からの江戸切子職人三代目。「跡を継ごう、と思ったのが高校二年生くらいの時。小さいころから家にいた職人さんたちと遊んでいたので、自然とそういう気持ちになりましたね」。

　小林さんの家は『一品もの』制作が多く、評価も高くてウデのいい職人さんが数多くいたとのこと。「この仕事についてからは、父というより、そうしたベテランの職人さんの背中を見て勉強しました。手元を見たり、作品を見たりして『盗む』感じですね。最初の10年間は本当に一所懸命でした」。

　当時、江戸切子職人として一人前になるには、仕事場の掃除から

始まって、使う砂や道具の管理、磨きの仕事を経て、粗摺りまでに7、8年かかる、といわれていたそうです。「今は、ダイヤモンドホイールなどの登場もあり、道具が進化したことで、技術の習得はより早くできるようになりました。でも、ものづくりにこだわる〝職人魂〟のようなものは、失ってはいけないと思います。一方で、それにより切子の可能性も広がっていますから、これからの職人はもっと柔軟な発想で、いろいろなことを考えていく必要があると思います」と語る小林さん。学校などで特別講師として教えることもあり、若い世代には大いに期待していると語ります。

ところで、実は既に〝四代目〟が修行中。長男の昂平さんです。

今年大学を卒業後、切子の道に。

「この道に進もう、と思ったきっかけは数え切れないほどありますが、中でも江戸切子には夢がある、夢中になれるものがあると感じたことが大きかったですね。僕も小さい頃から仕事場で遊んでいて、切子は身近だったのですが、実は今、仕事として取り組んでみて『大変なことになったな』と思っています。早く父に追いつきたい、と思っていますが、随分先になりそうです」。

職人のDNAがしっかりと、ここで受け継がれているようです。

The skill of Mr. Kobayashi is to engrave intricate patterns. A beautiful chrysanthemum crest is engraved on the base. The works of Mr. Kobayashi have also been adopted as presents to foreign dignitaries.

細雕精緻的花樣是小林先生的專長。底邊雕飾著美麗的菊花紋。小林先生的作品也常被選用為贈予外國貴賓的禮品。

精緻な模様を刻む小林さんのワザ。底辺には美しい菊花紋が。小林さんの作品は海外の要人への贈り物にも採用されています。

職人はやはり目が大切、と語る小林さん。鋭いまなざしが作品を見つめます。

Mr. Kobayashi explains that "Of course eyes are important for craftsmen." His sharp gaze goes over the object.

小林先生說，眼睛是工匠最重要的工具。尖銳的目光可以好好審視作品。

繊細な菊籠目紋。小林さんの得意とするところです。

A delicate chrysanthemum woven-bamboo pattern crest.
This is a specialty of Mr. Kobayashi.

纖細的菊籠目紋。這是小林先生擅長之處。

三番掛けの段階でつかう500番と呼ばれる細かい目のダイヤモンドホイール。このダイヤモンドホイールの登場により、より複雑なデザインが可能になりました。

The fine turn of a No.500 diamond wheel is used for third grade grinding. The arrival of this diamond wheel has led to ever more complicated designs becoming possible.

在第三階段所使用的鑽石砂輪，其磨石規格較細，通稱為500號。利用這台砂輪可以設計出更複雜細緻的花樣。

Freely draw out the attraction of the raw material,
The skill of an Edo Kiriko craftsman shines bright

The rainy season of June is over and it is already summer. Glasswork brings us a respite from the summer heat. On this occasion, we interviewed craftsmen of Edo Kiriko in the field of glass. Our first interviewee is Yoshiro Kobayashi. He is the Board Chairman of Tokyo Cut Glass Industry Cooperative. This is an association for Edo Kiriko. Mr. Kobayashi is a third generation Edo Kiriko craftsman. His grandfather was the first. "It was when I was in the second grade of high school that I decided I was going to continue the family business. From when I was little, I spent my time around craftsmen in our house and so I think it was only natural that I developed these feelings."

In the Kobayashi household there were many one-off works and a great number of highly skilled and highly regarded craftsmen. "Rather than my father, I learned about this job from watching veteran craftsmen at work. Following their examples and observing their works is kind of like having a feeling of stealing. The first ten years I really tried my hardest."

In order to come of age as an Edo Kiriko craftsman at that time, I was told that it takes seven to eight years; from starting with cleaning the workplace, managing the sand and tools to be used and working at the job of polishing, to the task of rough grinding. Mr. Kobayashi told us, "Nowadays, diamond wheels and the like have appeared on the scene and with advances in tools, it has become much faster to acquire the technical skills required. However, I think we must not lose what is kind of like the "soul of the craftsman" which is a perfectionist when it comes to craftsmanship. On the other hand, besides this, from the expanding possibilities of Kiriko, I think it is important that craftsmen, now and in the future, use even more flexible concepts to consider a variety of angles." He tells us that he also teaches as a special lecturer at schools and other places and that he has great hopes about the younger generation.

In fact, the fourth generation Kobayashi Edo Kiriko craftsman is already in the middle of learning the trade. This is his eldest son, Kouhei. After graduating university this year, he will take up the path of Kiriko.

"There are countless motivations why I wanted to follow this path, but I think chief among them is the feeling that without even really being aware of it, Edo Kiriko is something that I have become very familiar and enthusiastic about. I too played around in the work site from when I was very young and so Kiriko was very close to me. In fact, at present I think trying to come to grips with it as an actual job is something that is really difficult for me. I want to catch up with my father as soon as possible, but he seems to be a long way in the distance."

It seems as if the craftsman gene has truly been handed down from father to son.

將素材的魅力發揮到淋漓盡致，江戶雕花玻璃工匠的絕技使其綻放異彩

六月的梅雨季過後就是盛夏。玻璃雕花工藝為炎炎夏日帶來清爽感受。這次採訪了多位江戶雕花玻璃的工匠。最先拜訪的是擔任東京雕花玻璃工業同業工會理事長一職的小林淑郎先生。小林先生是從祖父那代算起第三代的江戶雕花玻璃工匠。「我是在高中二年級的時候決心要繼承家業的。因為我從小就跟家裡的工匠們玩在一起，自然而然地就有了這樣的念頭」。

小林先生家中有許多『絕世之作』，還聽說有多位評價高、手藝又精的工匠。「在開始進入這行後，並不是從我父親，而是看著工匠們熟練的動作學功夫的。一邊觀察他們的手部動作，一邊觀賞作品，就像是『偷學』來的。尤其剛開始的10年我真的是非常拼命」。

當時要成為獨當一面的江戶雕花玻璃工匠，要先從打掃工作室開始，透過管理整頓使用的砂石或工具，以及專致於研磨工作，然後到粗磨為止據說要耗上7、8年的時間。小林先生提到：「現在有鑽石砂輪及其他新工具可用，技術的學習時間比以前快多了。不過我認為絕不能失去創作所應堅持的「工匠精神」。另一方面，因為這使得江戶雕花玻璃的發展性更廣泛，我認為今後工匠應該以有靈活的構思，以便多方面聯想各種情況」。由於在學校擔任特別講師，小林先生說到他對年輕一代抱持著很大的期望。

說到這裡，其實「第四代」長男昂平已經開始在學功夫了。今年大學畢業後，他就要步上江戶雕花玻璃這條路。

「讓我想走這條路的契機多到數不清，其中最主要的原因是我覺得江戶雕花玻璃充滿夢想，有著使人為之著迷的魅力。我從小就在工房裡玩耍，對我而言江戶雕花玻璃並不陌生，事實上我開始從事這一行之後才知道『這工作還蠻辛苦的』。雖然很早日趕上我父親，不過看來還有很長的一段時間」。

看起來工匠的DNA確實在這裡完全地傳承下來了。

親から子へと、小林家では江戸切子職人の匠のワザが代々継承されています。

From parent to child; In the Kobayashi household the skills and techniques of Edo Kiriko craftsmen are handed down from generation to generation.

父親傳承給兒子，小林家讓江戶雕花玻璃的工匠技藝得以代代傳承。

連絡先／「江戸切子 小林」（有限会社小林硝子工芸所）　住所／東京都江東区猿江2-9-6
電話／03-3631-6457　営業時間／9:00〜18:00　定休日／日曜・祝日
HP／https://www.edokiriko1908.com

Contact information: Edo Kiriko Kobayashi (Kobayashi Glass Crafts Limited),　Address: 2-9-6 Sarue, Koutou-ku, Tokyo
Telephone: 03-3631-6457,　Opening hours: 9:00 – 18:00,　Closed days: Sundays and public holidays
https://www.edokiriko1908.com

聯絡處／「江戶雕花玻璃 小林」（小林玻璃工藝所有限公司）　地址／東京都江東區猿江2-9-6
電話／03-3631-6457　營業時間／9:00〜18:00　公休日／星期日・固定假日
https://www.edokiriko1908.com

江戸切子への夢を語る昂平さん。昂平さんは学生時代、学生作品展で学長賞を受賞したこともあるそうです。
Kouhei tells of his dream of Edo Kiriko. In his student days Kouhei also won the President's Award at a student exhibition.
昂平先生訴說著對於江戶雕花玻璃的夢想。據說他在學生時代就曾在學生作品展上得到校長獎。

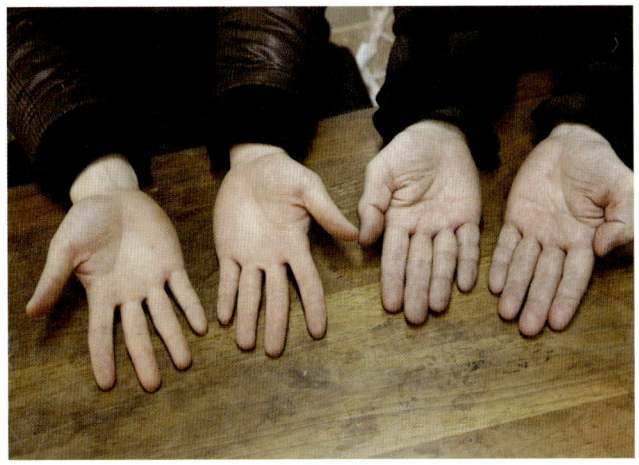

The craftsman gene flows through these hands.
內藏工匠DNA的手。

職人のDNAが流れる手。

淑郎さん（右）と長男の昂平さん（左）。
ふだんはとても仲の良さそうな親子です。

Yoshiro (right) and his eldest son, Kouhei (left).
It looks like father and son are usually on really good terms.

淑郎先生（右）與長男昂平（左）。
父子兩人平常相處就非常融洽。

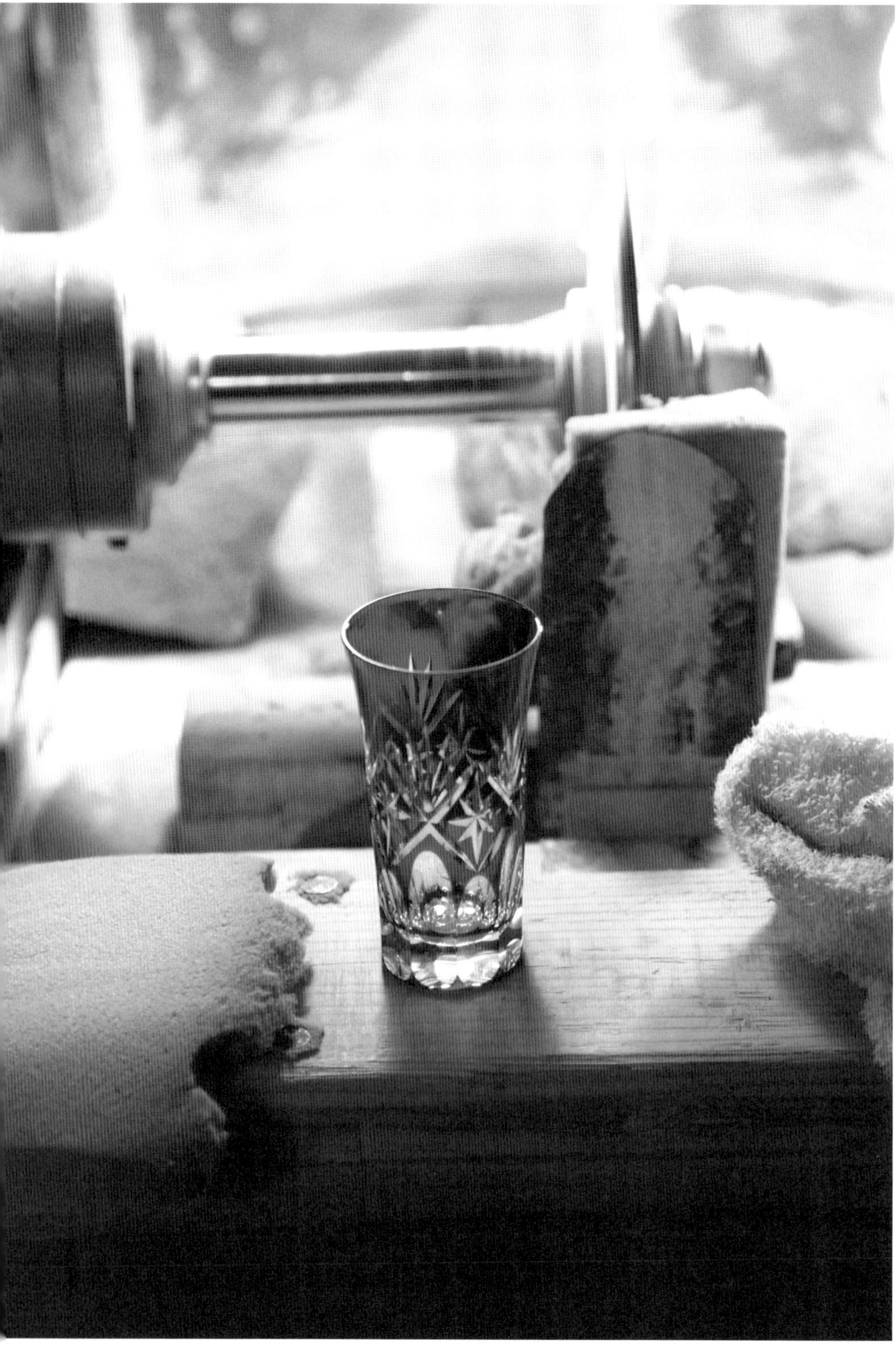

江戸切子の歴史

History of Edo Kiriko

江戶雕花玻璃的歷史

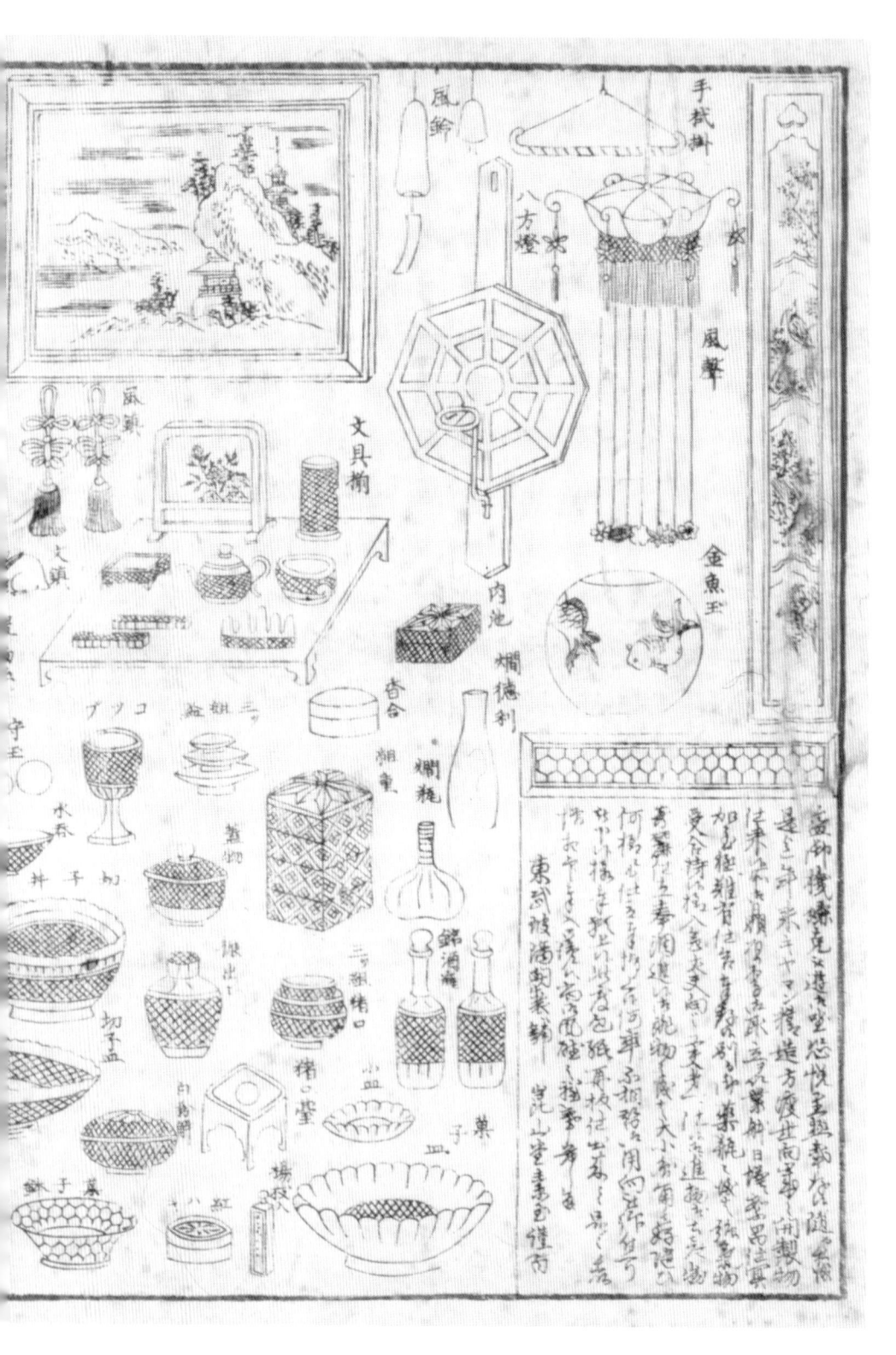

手拭掛
風鈴
八方燈
風琴
金魚玉
文具棚
風鎮
内池
燗徳利
香合
燗鍋
錦袋編
巣子皿
三ツ組猪口
猪口臺
小皿
菓子皿

黄銅機器並瓦斯燈等器具類
遠近新來ナランヤマン模造方度世而萬一開製物
法来之ルガ頗ル書之以テ巧ニ其品廉ニ
加之経濟資任任各製其到達品出來
更ニ令待得候入貮更向薬師合數寄物
同御座候儀と奉存候様御披露被下度御願申候
何卒其様被仰付被成下候樣仰出候御用向
其御許様之程寄席と奉存候依而願之通
東叡被連邸兼輔
崑山堂主人白健而

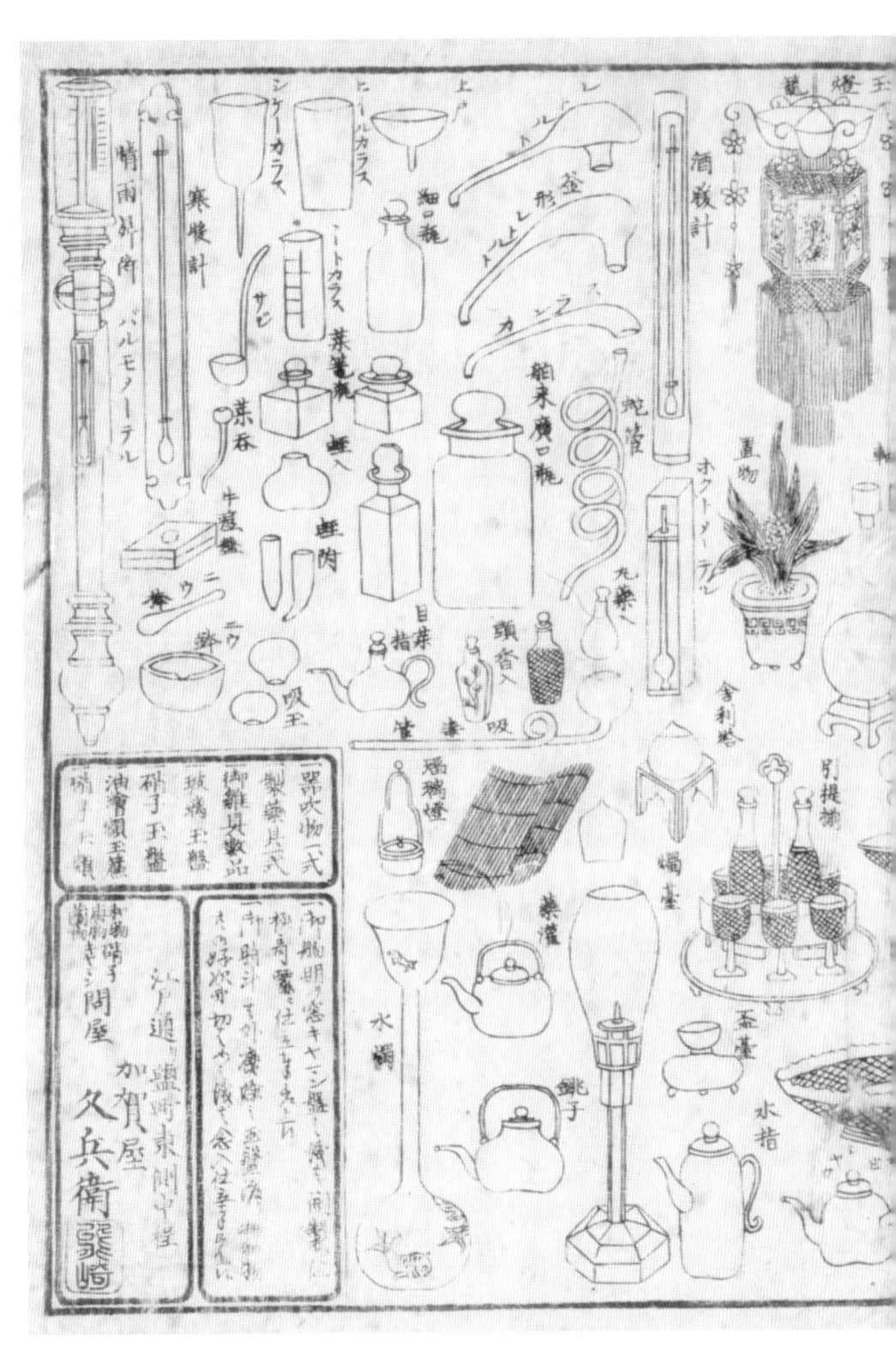

（図版：ガラス器具類・薬品瓶・ランプ等の図）

ラベル（図中）：
- 晴雨計 バルモメートル
- 寒暖計
- コルトカラス
- 細口瓶
- シケーカラス
- ヒールカラス
- 上
- レトルト形
- 釜
- レトルト
- カンニス
- 筒験計
- 籠燈
- 葉筌瓶
- 葉呑
- サジ
- 無入
- 生肉
- 舶来廣口瓶
- 蛇管
- 九藥
- オクトメートル
- 置物
- ウニ
- 蜂
- ニウ
- 吸玉
- 目床
- 指套
- 頭香入
- 吸
- 簷
- 番
- 舍利塔
- 福禄燈
- 引提燈
- 燭臺
- 盃臺
- 藥罐
- 水鍋
- 銚子
- 水指

一器吹物一式
製藥具数品
御雛具数品
硝子玉盤
玻璃玉盤
油壺類玉簾
硝子類

（略）

江戸通り鹽町東門中程
加賀屋
久兵衛

英国のカットグラスを模したのが起源。
見事な切子にペリーも驚愕

天保5年（1834年）に、江戸大伝馬町でビードロ問屋を営んでいた加賀屋久兵衛という人物が、英国製のカットグラスを模してガラスの表面に彫刻を施したのが、江戸切子の始まりと言われています。また、幕末に黒船で来航したペリー提督が、加賀屋から献上された ガラス瓶の見事な切子に驚いたという逸話も伝えられています。

明治15年（1882年）には、工部省品川工作所が西洋式カット及び摺模様の技術者エマヌエル・ホープトマンをイギリスより招き、技術を伝習させたそうです。現代に伝わる精巧なカットの技法の多くは、この時に始まったとされています。その後、震災・戦災ほか幾多の困難はあったものの、江戸時代からの切子の伝統は絶えることなく、今日まで長い間守られてきました。

ちなみにですが、荒川沿いの下町を中心に「江戸切子」が発展したのは、ガラスの主な材料である珪石を、当時の珪石の採掘地、福島から荒川沿いの下町に船で運んでいたためだそうです。

(P24-25) 医療器具から食器まで、さまざまな硝子製品が描かれた「加賀屋久兵衛引札」。切子が施された商品も多く見受けられます。このことから、江戸後期には江戸切子が商品として流通していたことが分かります。
加賀屋久兵衛引札（再版）　江戸後期（1826～1850）／びいどろ史料庫

(P. 24-25) From medical instruments to tableware; various glass products are depicted on a handbill of Kyubei Kagaya. We can see that many products have had Kiriko applied to them. From this, we can deduce that in the late Edo period, Edo Kiriko was being distributed as a product.
Handbill of Kyubei Kagaya (reprint) late Edo period (1826-1850) / Biidoro Historical Archives

(P24-25) 從醫療器具到餐具，各種玻璃製品都雕有「加賀屋久兵衛引札」。另外也可見到許多雕花玻璃的商品。因此可得知，在江戶後期時江戶雕花玻璃是一種流通於市的商品。
加賀屋久兵衛引札（再版）　江戶後期（1826～1850）／Biidoro史料庫

The origins of Edo Kiriko are found in imitations of British cut glass,
The magnificent Kiriko surprised even Commodore Perry
It is said that Edo Kiriko started in 1834 when a man called Kyubei Kagaya, who ran a glass wholesale store in Edo Odenmacho, imitated British-made cut glass and applied engraving to the surface of glass. Furthermore, legend tells that U.S. Commodore Perry, the man whose arrival of black ships in the closing days of the Tokugawa shogunate helped open up Japan in 1852, was surprised with a beautiful Kiriko glass bottle presented to him by Kagaya.
In 1882, the Ministry of Works Shinagawa Engineering Center invited from Britain a technical expert of western style cut glass and printed patterns, Emanuel Hoputoman, so that they could learn these techniques. Many of the sophisticated cutting techniques that have been handed down today were started at this time. Afterwards, despite the numerous difficulties in addition to earthquakes and wars, the traditions of Kiriko from the Edo period have not died out, but instead have been preserved to this day.
Incidentally, the development of Edo Kiriko was centered on the downtown area along the Arakawa River, because the main material in glass, silica, was transported by ship from Fukushima, the mining area of silica at that time, to downtown Tokyo along the Arakawa River.

起源於英國的雕花玻璃。
完美的雕花玻璃讓培里提督也讚嘆不已
天保5年（1834年）在江戶大傳馬町有位經營玻璃的批發商，名叫加賀屋久兵衛，他仿照英國製的雕花玻璃在玻璃表面進行雕飾，被認為是江戶雕花玻璃的開端。此外也流傳幕末時搭乘黑船前來的培里提督，看到加賀屋贈送的玻璃瓶花樣精美而讚嘆不已的軼事。
在明治15年（1882年），工部省品川工事所從英國聘請西式雕花與渲染技師伊曼紐爾・霍普托曼（Emanuel Hoputoman）傳授技藝。據說許多傳承至今的精巧雕花技藝都是始於此時。後來雖經歷震災、戰爭和其他諸多苦難，源自江戶時代的雕花玻璃傳統並沒有斷絕，一直被保存維持至今。
附帶一提，「江戶雕花玻璃」會以荒川沿岸的下町為中心發展，乃是因玻璃的主要原料矽石是在福島開採的，當時要用船從福島運至荒川沿岸的下町之故。

江戸切子の年表

Timeline of Edo Kiriko
江戶雕花玻璃的年表

1543
種子島へポルトガル船が漂着

A Portuguese ship drifts ashore at Tanegashima, in southern Japan.

葡萄牙商船漂流至種子島。

1549
宣教師フランシスコ・ザビエルが訪日。ガラス文化が再び始まる

The missionary Francisco de Xavier visits Japan. Glass culture starts again.

傳教師法蘭西斯克・薩威爾訪日。玻璃文化再度興起。

1711頃
江戸でガラスの製造が始まる

The manufacture of glass begins in Edo.

在江戶開始玻璃製造工業。

1834
江戸大伝馬町でビードロ問屋を営む加賀屋久兵衛が、無色のガラスにカットを施す。江戸切子が誕生

Kyubei Kagaya, who ran a glass wholesale store in Edo Odenmacho, applies cutting to colorless glass. Edo Kiriko is born.

在江戶大傳馬町經營玻璃批發的加賀屋久兵衛，他在無色的玻璃上施加雕飾，江戶雕花玻璃自此誕生。

1846
江戸のガラス技術が薩摩に伝わる。薩摩切子が誕生

The glass techniques of Edo are introduced into Satsuma (an ancient province located in present-day Kagoshima prefecture). Satsuma Kiriko is born.

江戶玻璃技藝傳至薩摩，誕生了薩摩雕花玻璃。

1855
薩摩藩主・島津斉彬がガラス製造所を拡張し「集成館」と命名

The daimyō (feudal lord) of Satsuma Nariakira Shimazu expands his glass factory and names it Shuuseikan.

薩摩藩主・島津齊彬擴大玻璃製造工廠，並命名為「集成館」。

1863
薩英戦争で「集成館」焼失

The Shuuseikan is destroyed by fire in the Anglo-Satsuma War.

「集成館」在薩英戰爭中燒毀。

1873
ウィーン万国博覧会へ加賀屋がガラス器を出品

Kagaya exhibits his glassware at the Vienna World Exhibition.

加賀屋在維也納萬國博覽會中展出玻璃器皿。

1876
工部省が「品川工作所」を設立。ヨーロッパの新しい技術が導入される

The Ministry of Works establishes the Shinagawa Engineering Center. New European techniques are introduced.

工部省設立「品川工作所」，引進歐洲的最新技術。

1882
イギリス人技師エマヌエル・ホープトマンによって、伝習生に切子の技術が伝えられる

Through the British technical expert Emanuel Hoputoman (Emanuel Hoputoman) students learned about the techniques of Kiriko.

英國工藝技師伊曼紐爾・霍普托曼（Emanuel Hoputoman）把雕花玻璃的技術傳授給研習學徒。

29

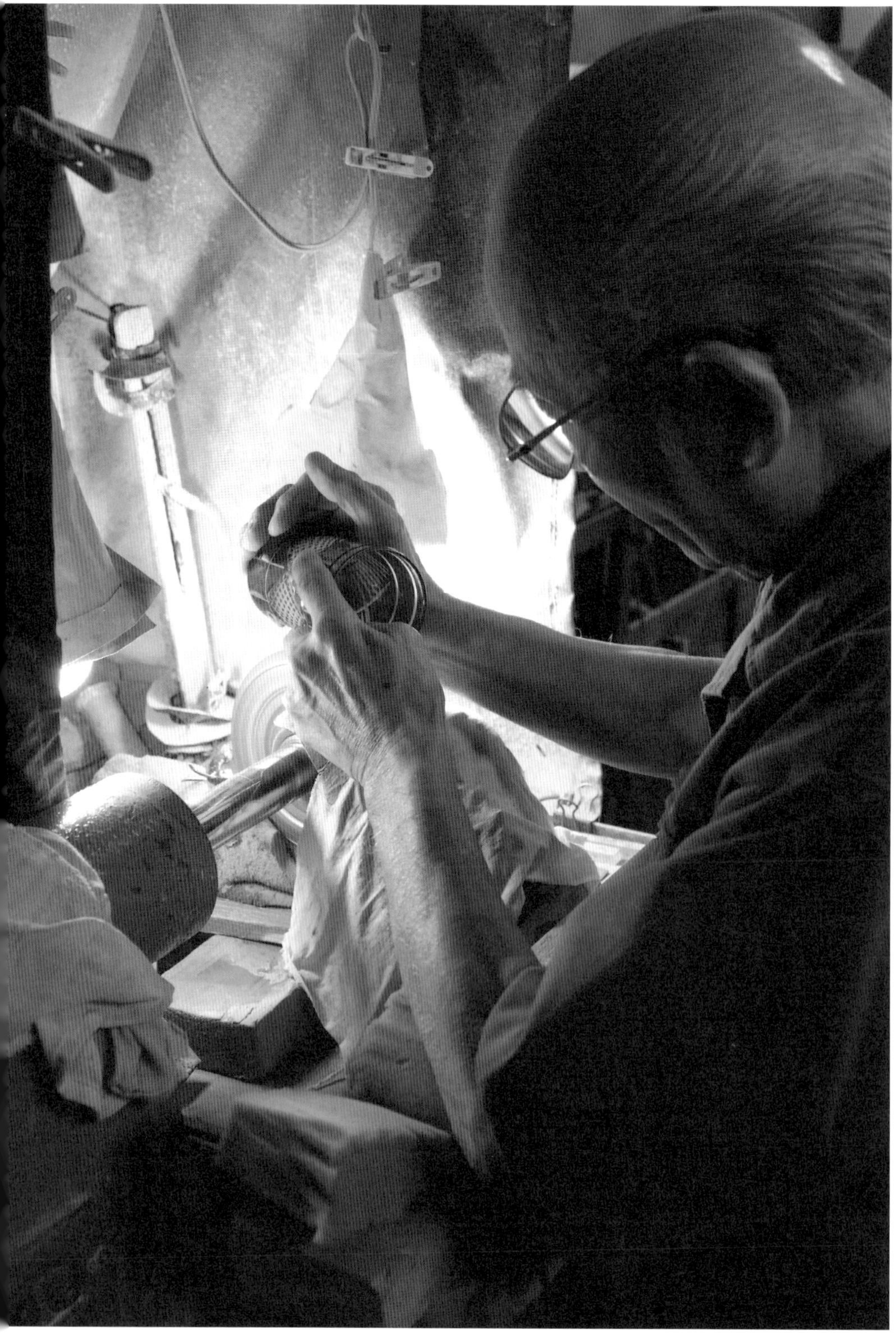

町工場に勤める

Working in a Small Factory.

在町廠工作

株式会社 清水硝子
Shimizu Glass Corporation
清水玻璃股份有限公司

1923年（大正12年）創業の清水硝子は、江戸切子町工場のなかでも歴史のある工場です。ここには職人歴60年という大ベテランの匠から、OLを辞めて職人の世界に飛び込んで数年の、さまざまなキャリアの江戸切子職人が働いています。後継者が不足する伝統工芸の世界で、世代を超えて始まったワザの伝承。その実際を取材させていただきました。

プロフィール／1923年（大正12年）本所菊川町に清水硝子加工場を創業。クリスタル硝子・江戸切子のカットグラス、研磨加工及び製造・販売を行う。受託加工・制作依頼・記念品・特注品・OEMにも対応。ガラス製品の欠け・傷などの修理も行う。※詳しくはホームページでご確認ください。

Shimizu Glass was established in 1923 and is a factory that has its place in history among Edo Kiriko small factories. Edo Kiriko craftsmen with a variety of careers work at this factory; from veteran craftsmen with 60 years of experience in the industry, to women who have been working here for a few years after quitting their previous jobs as administrative assistants and then leaping into the world of craftsmen. In the world of traditional crafts where there is a lack of people willing to take up this line of work, the handing down of these techniques has started to go beyond the generations.
We were allowed to visit and see for ourselves this factory.

清水玻璃創業於1923年（大正12年），即使在多家江戶雕花玻璃的町工廠之中也算是頗具歷史的工廠。這裡有多位不同背景的江戶雕花玻璃工匠，有60年資歷的老師傅，也有辭掉辦公室工作投入工匠世界的女性。在新手不足的傳統工藝世界裡，傳承著超越世代的絕技。就讓我們好好來實地探訪。

簡介／1923年（大正12年）清水玻璃加工廠在本所菊川町創業。開始水晶玻璃、江戶雕花玻璃的研磨加工、製造與銷售。另外也接受委託加工、客製化加工、紀念品、特別訂單、OEM等。也能修復玻璃製品的缺角、損傷等。※詳情請上網確認。

Profile: The Shimizu Glass Factory was established in Honjo Kikugawa-chou in 1923. This factory performs cut glass of crystal glass and Edo Kiriko, the polishing process and manufacturing and sales. The factory also supports contract processing, commissioned works, mementos, special orders and original equipment manufacturing. They can also repair cracks and chips to glass products. *For more details, please visit their website.

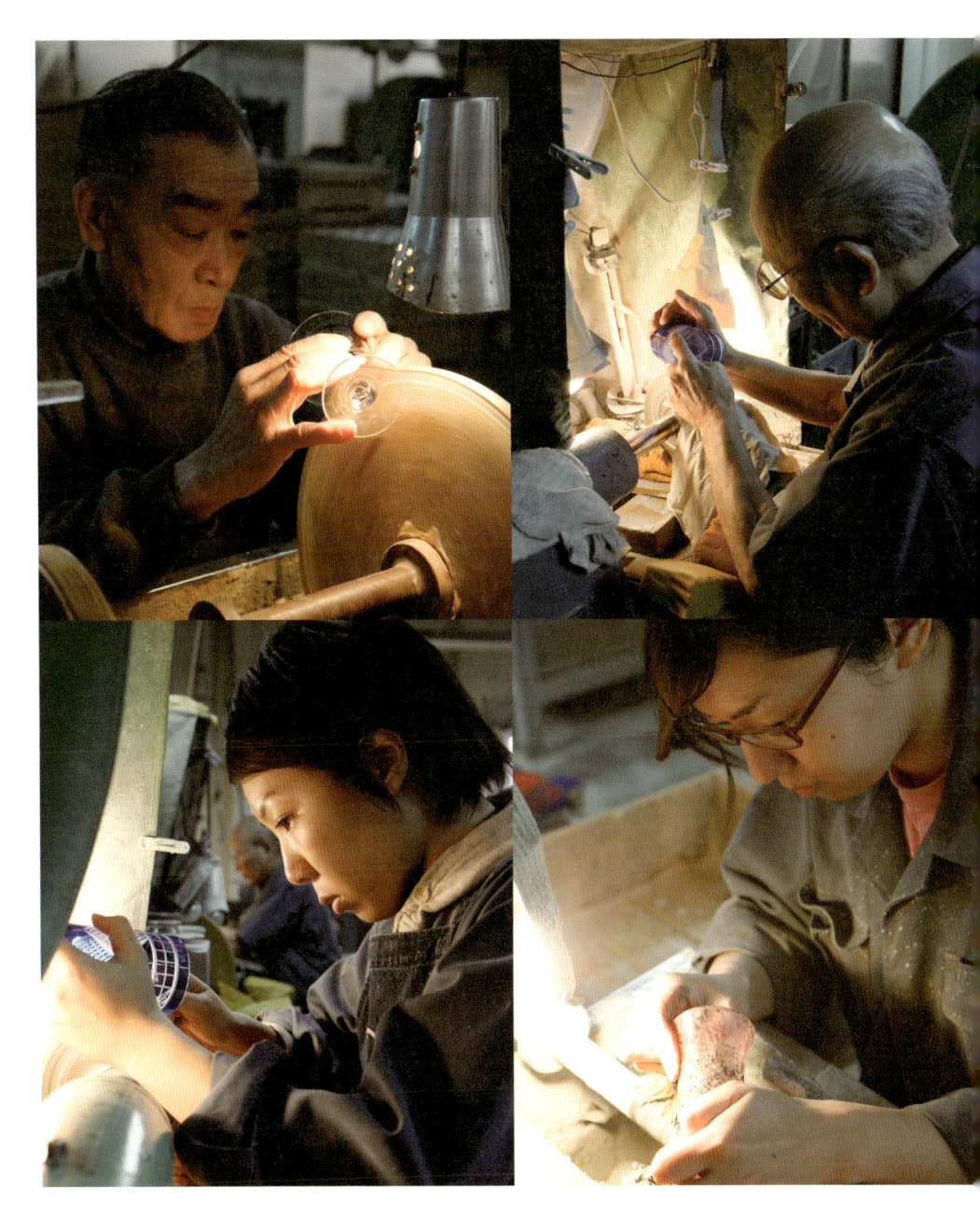

歴史の古い町工場、清水硝子ではさまざまなキャリアの職人が腕を磨いています。
中宮涼子さん（写真左下）は、2019年に女性として初めて、日本の伝統工芸士に認定されました。

At the historical small factory of Shimizu Glass, craftsmen with a variety of careers are honing their techniques.
Ryoko Nakamiya (pictured bottom left) became the first woman to be certified as a traditional craftsman in Japan in 2019.

清水玻璃，這是一家頗具歷史的町工廠，有多位不同背景的工匠在此磨練學藝。
2019年，中宮涼子女士（照片左下方）被認定為日本第一位女性傳統工藝士。

モノづくりに挑戦する若い感性を、職人の経験とワザが育てる

「人はどうみているか知りませんが、まだ、自分を一人前とは思っていません」。そう語るのは清水硝子の工場長・三田隆三さん。とは言うものの、三田さんは職人歴60年。「15歳の時に先輩に誘われてこの道に入りました。当初は親方や先輩に厳しく指導されて、泣いたこともありました。切子は水を使いますので、空調の無かった当時の冬はとても辛かったですね。切子は一個一個すべてが手づくりですから、同じものをつくっても、季節や、日々の天候、午前につくったか午後につくったか、時には体調などで仕上がりが異なってしまう場合があります。それが味でもあるのですが、職人としては全く同じものが仕上がらなくてはだめではないか、とも思います」と自らにも厳しい目を向けます。

そんな三田さんのもと、清水硝子では若い『職人の卵』が育っています。今回はその中で、"職人歴"2年目の青山弥生さんと1年目の長島尚子さんにお話をうかがいました。

清水硝子のショールームで三田さんのお話をうかがいました。
工場長のもと生み出されたオリジナル商品が数多く展示されていました。
三田さんは、2014年に東京都優秀技能者（東京マイスター）として認定されました。

I listened to Mr. Mita's story at the showroom of Shimizu Glass. There were many original products on display that had been produced under the factory manager. Mita was certified as a Tokyo master technician (Tokyo Meister) in 2014.

我們在清水玻璃的展示廳採訪到三田先生。這裡展示許多源自於三田廠長的原創商品。
2014年，三田先生被認定為東京都優秀技能者（東京巨匠）。

「切子の魅力は"輝き"。最初の、まだ何も模様のない状態から、次第に仕上がっていって、最後に磨きをかけられて輝きを放った時には、自分でも『いいな』と思います」と三田さんは語ります。

"The attraction of Kiriko is its radiance. From the beginning when the glass still has no pattern at all, as gradually it is finished, until the final polishing; when the piece gives off its radiance, even I think to myself 'That's good'" says Mr. Mita.

三田先生說「玻璃雕花的魅力在於"光采"。最初，從看不出模樣的狀態開始，慢慢地成形，最後研磨後綻放出耀眼的光采時，連自己都會感到『太好了』」。

三田さんの手。
難しいこともとても
簡単そうにやってしまうのが、
職人歴60年のワザでしょうか。

Mr. Mita's hands. He makes even something difficult look exceedingly easy, but then surely that is the skill of someone with 60 years of experience.

三田先生的手。即使是困難的步驟也能輕易完成，這就是60年資歷所孕育出來的絕技吧。

This is Ms. Nagashima who has one year of experience as a craftsman. Work such as cleaning the workplace and carrying the product to the next process are also a very important job. Ms. Nagashima starts with these simple tasks and will gradually then take up the challenge of more difficult work.

工匠資歷第一年的長島小姐。整理工作環境或把作品搬運到下一步製程等，這些都是重要的任務。從簡單的項目開始慢慢地循序漸進。

職人歴1年目の長島さん。仕事場の片付けや製品を次の工程に運んだりするのも大切な仕事。簡単なものから徐々に仕事に取り組んでいます。

職人歴2年目の青山さん。最初は磨きなどの工程から始め、今は既に多くの仕事を任されるようになっています。

This is Ms. Aoyama who has one year of experience as a craftsman. She started on processes such as polishing and now she has already been entrusted with many other jobs.

工匠資歷第二年的青山先生。最初由研磨製程開始，現在已經可以勝任很多其他項目了。

37

青山さんも長島さんも葛飾区の『伝統工芸職人弟子入り支援事業』※を利用し、清水硝子に入ってきました。青山さんは学校でプロダクトデザインを勉強。ここに来る前はインテリア用のカーテンなどの企画デザインをする仕事をしていたそうです。「企業の一部署で働いていると、その年や季節の流行に合わせ、とても早いサイクルで製品が流れていきます。もっとじっくり、そして長く使ってもらえるモノづくりがしたくて、この道に飛び込んできました」。

一方、長島さんはサービス関連の仕事からの挑戦。「夏休みの工作とか、とても好きだったのです。いつかはモノづくりの仕事がしたいと思っていました。以前勤めていた会社は大きな会社で、居心地も悪くなかったのですが、今はやっぱり、こっちの方が性に合っているな、と思っています」。

ふたりとも、ガラスについての知識や経験は全くなかったそうですが、ガラスという素材には興味を持っていたそう。いまは職人への道を一歩一歩、歩み始めています。工場長の三田さんは、そんなふたりを温かい目で見守っています。「若い人の持つ感性やデザインのセンスは、大切にしていきたいと思います。もちろん、伝統の技術や道具の選択、使い方などは時間をかけて習得していかなければなりませんが、より新しいモノづくりを目指して欲しい。私も負けないようさらにいいモノづくりに挑戦していきたいと思います」。

※葛飾区の制度は平成21年度の募集をもって終了しています。

連絡先／株式会社清水硝子　住所／東京都葛飾区堀切4-64-7（ショールーム有。展示即売も行なっています）
電話／03-3690-1205　営業時間／8:00〜17:00　定休日／土曜・日曜・祝日
HP／http://www2u.biglobe.ne.jp/~kirikoya/

Contact information: Shimizu Glass Corporation,　Address: 4-64-7 Horikiri, Katsushika-ku, Tokyo
(There is a showroom. There is also an exhibition and sales.)
Telephone: 03-3631-6457,　Opening hours: 9:00 – 18:00,　Closed days: Sundays and public holidays
http://www2u.biglobe.ne.jp/~kirikoya/

聯絡處／清水玻璃股份有限公司　地址／東京都葛飾區堀切4-64-7（有展示廳。也同時進行現場銷售）
電話／03-3690-1205　營業時間／8:00〜17:00　公休日／星期六・星期日・固定假日
http://www2u.biglobe.ne.jp/~kirikoya/

The experience and techniques of craftsmen develop the young senses of those that take up craftsmanship

"However people look at me, I don't know , but I cannot see myself as having completely come of age." These are the words of Ryuuzou Mita, the Factory Manager at Shimizu Glass. Although he says this, Mr. Mita is a person with 60 years' experience as a craftsman. "When I was 15 years old, an older craftsman encouraged me to take up this line of work. At first, my master and my older colleagues were very strict in their guidance and there were times when I was reduced to tears. Kiriko uses water, so at that time in winter when there was no air conditioning, it was really tough. Kiriko is all handmade, piece by piece, and so even when making the same object it is possible that the season, the daily weather, whether it is made in the morning or whether it is made in the afternoon and occasionally even the craftsman's physical condition can all cause a difference in the end product. This is the case even with experience, but as a craftsman I also wonder whether it is right to make a completely identical end product." These are the words of a man who strictly scrutinizes himself.

At Shimizu Glass under Mr. Mita, expert craftsmen in the making are being developed. Of these protégés, we spoke to Yayoi Aoyama who has two years' experience as a craftsman and Naoko Nagashima with one year's experience.

Both Ms. Aoyama and Ms. Nagashima used the Support Program for Apprentices of Traditional Crafts offered by the local government of Katsushika-ku* to join Shimizu Glass. Ms. Aoyama studied product design at school. Before coming here she held a job planning and designing curtains and the like. "When working at that position I had to meet the fashions of that year or that season and the product cycle was very short. I wanted to work with products that are more deliberate and which will be used for a long time and so I jumped into this line of work."

On the other hand, Ms. Nagashima has come to this job from the service sector. "I worked in construction in summer and I really liked it. I thought that one day I would like to do a job connected with craftsmanship. The company that I worked at previously was a really big firm and so I didn't really fit in there, but now I think that, of course, here is somewhere that I am much better suited to."

Both women had no knowledge or experience when it came to glass, but they did possess an interest in the raw material of glass. Now, they have started, step by step, on the road to becoming craftsmen. The factory manager Mr. Mita watches over these two with warm eyes. "I hope that the sense young people possess and the sense of design will be cherished. Of course, the traditional techniques, the choice of tools and the way to use them and other skills must take a long time to learn, but I hope they aim at an even newer craftsmanship. I too would like to challenge myself to never give up and set myself the task of making even better craftsmanship."

* The Katsushika-ku system is already closed to applications in the fiscal year 2009.

工匠的經驗與絕技培育著挑戰工藝的年輕感性

「別人怎麼想我不清楚，但我覺得自己還不能獨當一面」，說這句話的是清水玻璃的廠長‧三田隆三先生。雖說如此，三田先生已有60年工匠資歷。「15歲時受以前輩指引而進了這行。當初師傅和前輩的教導非常嚴格，我還曾經哭了好幾次。因為製作雕花玻璃要用水，在當年沒有暖氣的時代，冬天真的是苦不堪言。雕花玻璃每個都要以手工製作，即使做同樣的東西，因季節或天氣，甚至上午或下午，乃至於個人當天身體狀況的不同，所製作出來的作品也各有千秋。那算是其個別的風格，但我也會嚴以律己地想說，工匠的職責就是要能做出完全相同的作品，不是嗎？」

這就是三田先生，他們下正培育著清水玻璃的工匠新人。就讓我們來採訪工匠資歷第二年的青山彌生先生及第一年的長島尚子小姐。青山先生與長島小姐皆透過『傳統工藝拜師入門支援事業』，而拜師於清水玻璃門下。青山先生在學校學的是產品設計，來這裡之前做的是室內窗簾相關的企劃設計工作。「如果在企業的部署下做事，就會為了配合年度或季節流行，而讓產品的循環變得非常快。我想要專心製作能夠長久使用的物品，因此才決定步入這行的。」

另一方面，長島小姐則是脫離原本的服務業前來挑戰。「我很喜歡像是暑假的手工藝等的作業，所以一直想著總有一天要從事創造製作的行業。我以前是在一間大公司上班，雖然待遇不差，但總覺得還是這方面的工作比較適合我。」

據說最初這兩人對玻璃相關知識及經驗可說是一竅不通，單純只是對這種名為玻璃的素材感到興趣。然而他們現在正開始一步一步往工匠的方向邁進。三田廠長總是用溫暖的目光守護著他們兩人。「我想善用年輕人特有的感受、以及對設計的品味。當然，傳統的技藝和道具的選擇和使用方法，這些也必須花時間好好學習才行，但我還是希望她們能將視野放在製作更新穎的作品上。我也不會輕易認輸，我會努力挑戰以期待更好的作品。」

※葛飾區這項制度已在平成21年度最後一次實施後終止。

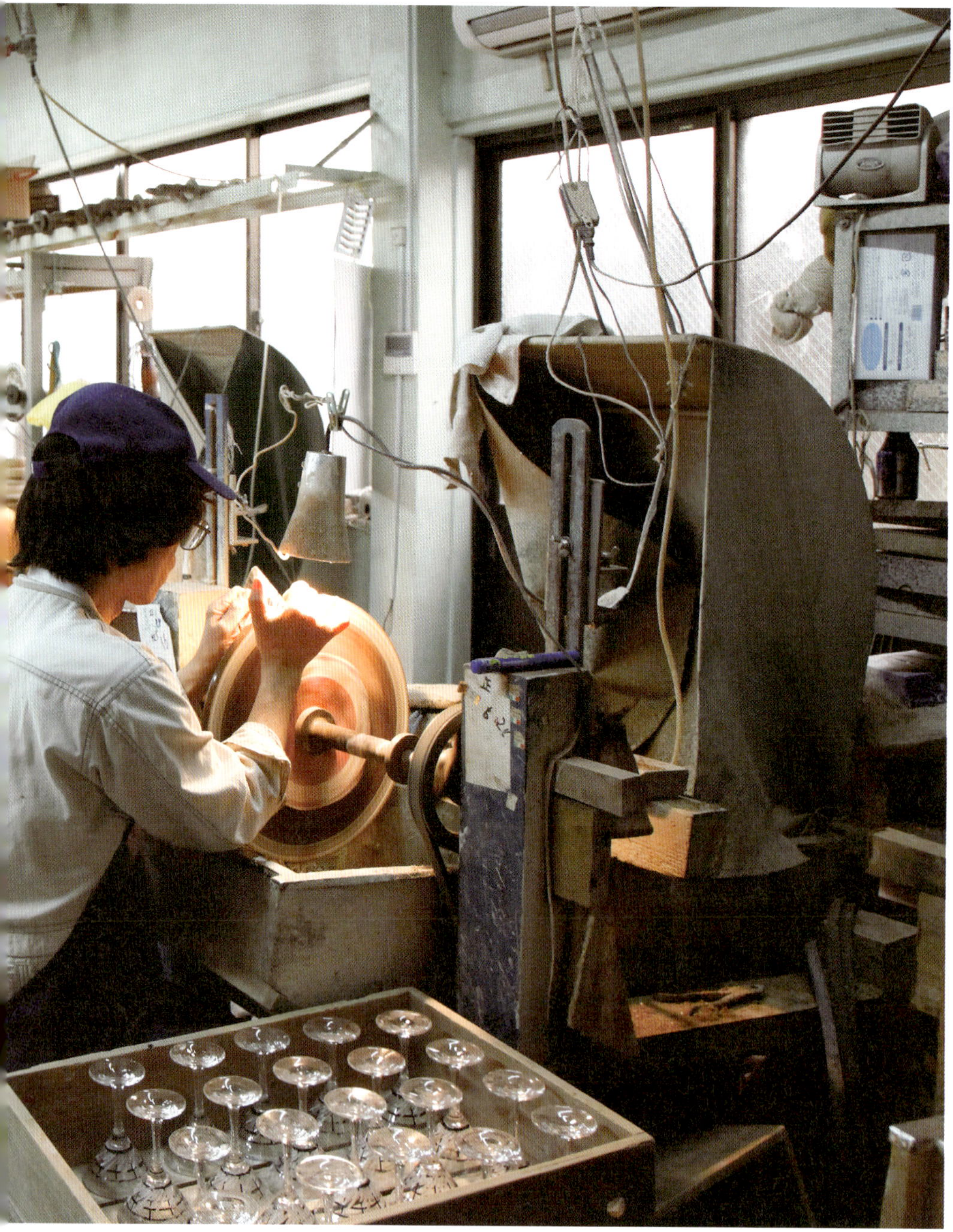

それぞれの職人が分業をしながら、江戸切子を仕上げていきます。

With each craftsman working on their own part of the process, the Edo Kiriko is completed.

工匠們依照製程分工作業，以完成江戸雕花玻璃的製作。

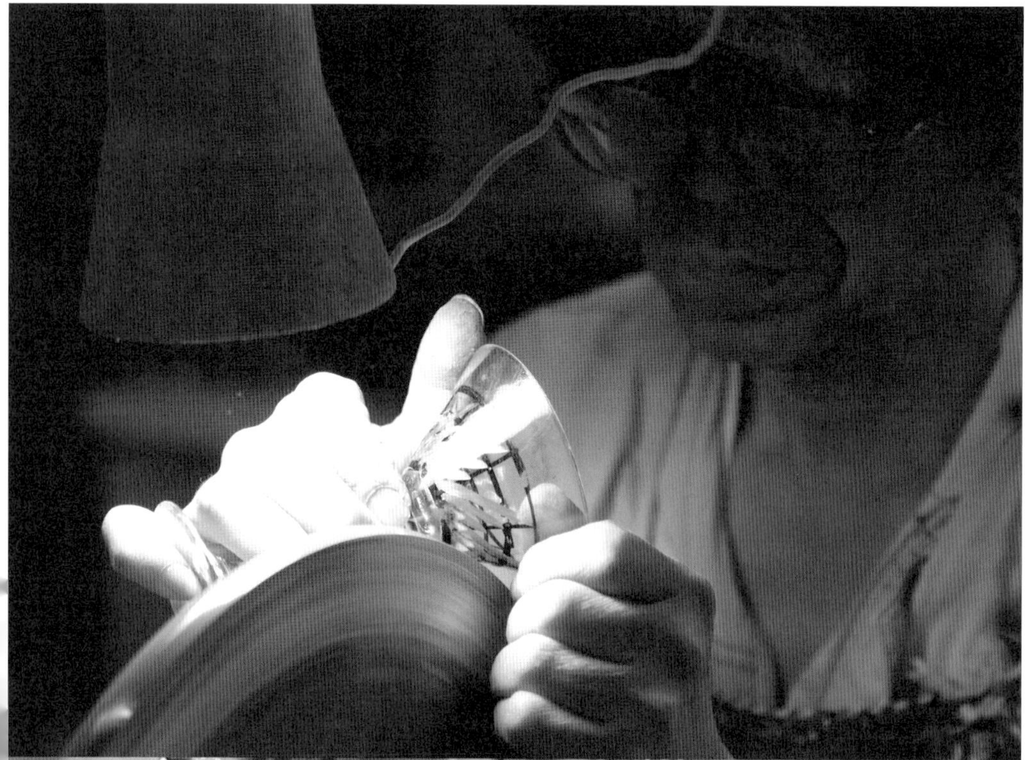

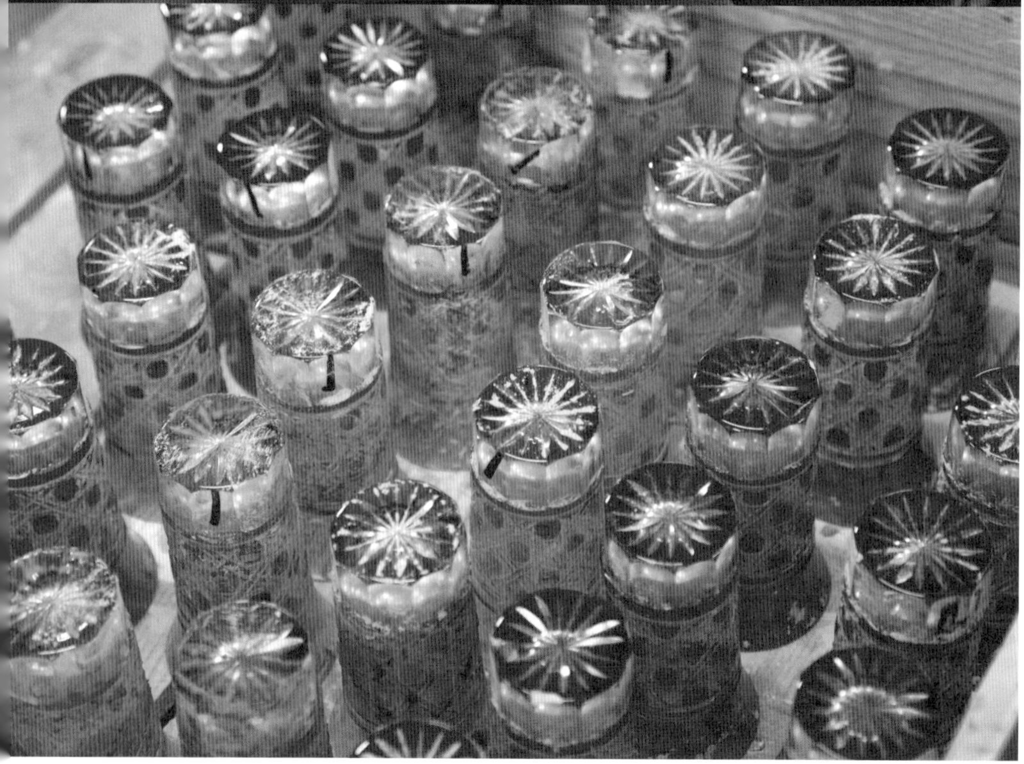

江戸切子のつくり方

The Way of Making Edo Kiriko

江戸雕花玻璃的製作方法

割り出し

Marking

構圖分割

ガラスの表面に図柄の目安となる印を付ける「割り出し」。下絵はなく、あとは職人のワザで模様を付けていきます。

筋彫り

Line engraving

描繪輪廓

The marking stage is where marks are affixed which will become the pattern of reference on the surface of the glass. Without a rough sketch, later the pattern will be affixed by the skill of the craftsman.

在玻璃表面做記號以預設圖案位置的「構圖分割」。
沒有底稿，圖樣繪製全憑工匠的技藝。

雕花玻璃由左圖開始依次成形。剛開始以100～170號左右較粗的鑽石砂輪進行粗磨，接著以300～500號慢慢磨出模樣（三番掛），再來用磨石讓表面呈現細滑質感（石掛）。最後，旋轉木盤、樹脂及毛氈布料，再沾上研磨劑即可磨出精美的色澤。（另一種作法是用藥品進行「酸磨」）。

From left to right; this Kiriko glass gradually takes shape. First, the glass undergoes a rough grind with a coarse diamond wheel of around No. 100-170. Next, with a No. 300-500 the shaving of the pattern further proceeds (third grade grinding). After this, the processed surface is finely smoothened with a grindstone (smoothing). Finally, a wooden board, resin, felt or something similar is rotated around with a polishing agent applied and when polished, a beautiful radiance is created (There is also a process called 'acid polishing' with chemicals).

粗摺り
Rough grind
粗磨

目の粗いダイヤモンドホイールでの粗摺り。大きな模様を始めに削っていきます。

石掛け
Smoothing
石磨

磨き
Polishing
細磨

The rough grind by the coarse diamond wheel. To begin with, the rough pattern will be shaved down.

以規格較粗的鑽石砂輪進行粗磨。自此削磨出大致的模樣。

左から次第に形になっていく切子。最初は100〜170番程度の目の粗いダイヤモンドホイールで粗摺りをし、次に300〜500番のものでさらに模様を削り進め（三番掛け）、次に砥石によって加工面を細かくなめらかに（石掛け）。最後に木盤や樹脂、フェルトなどを回転させ研磨剤をつけて磨くと、美しい輝きが生まれます（薬品による「酸磨き」という方法もあります）。

文様を削り出し、なめらかに研磨。
「磨き」工程は切子の魅力を左右

図案の配分を決め、図柄を入れる場所の目安となる印を付け、それを頼りに図柄の基準となる線を細く、そして浅く削ります。のちの加工で、微調整がしやすいように、仕上がり予定の4分の3程度の幅および深さに加工する「粗摺り」、「粗摺り」で付けた溝を頼りに、さらに細かい加工を施す「三番掛け」の工程を行ったあとは、「粗摺り」や「三番掛け」によって削りだした文様の形を整え、加工面を滑らかに研磨。「石掛け」は、削りの最終工程のため、丁寧に研磨します。

加工後、不透明な状態になっている表面を磨き、ガラス本来の透明感のある輝きを取り戻させます。どんなにカットが良くても、「磨き」次第では、切子の良さは引き立たないため、最終工程の「磨き」は、切子の魅力を左右する大切な工程となります。

削磨出圖樣後進行更細滑的研磨。
「細磨」這道製程足以左右雕花玻璃的整體魅力。

決定圖案的分佈格局後，在要上圖的位置做記號，靠此削出圖樣淺淺的基礎線。在往後的加工作業上，為了能容易微調，在預定完工的4分之3寬度和深度進行「粗磨」。按照「粗磨」刻上的溝，進行較細的「三番掛」加工，再用「粗磨」或「三番掛」調整已削出的紋樣，接著細磨加工面。「石磨」是削磨中的最後步驟，打磨要非常細心謹慎。

加工後，細磨呈現不透明的表面以回復玻璃原有的透明感。無論是多好的雕花，「細磨」這道步驟的優劣會決定雕花玻璃的好壞，所以最後的「細磨」是左右雕花玻璃魅力的重要製程。

The pattern is cut and the piece is ground smooth.
The polishing process determines the attraction of Kiriko
The distribution of the design is decided upon and marks are affixed that will become the reference points for where the pattern will be engraved. The lines that rely on these to form the basis of the pattern are finely drawn and are then shaved down to a shallow depth. In the later processing stages, in order to make it easy to carry out slight adjustments, a third grade grinding process is performed that applies a further refined process to the grooves that have been made by the rough grinding process which has been carried out to a width and depth that is around three quarters of the planned finish. After this, the shape of the pattern that has been ground down by the rough grind and the third grade grinding is arranged and then the processed finish is ground smooth. The smoothing process is a careful grind for the final process of shaving.

After processing, the surface, which has become opaque, is polished and a radiance that possesses the clarity of the original glass is restored. No matter how well the glass is cut, the quality of Kiriko is dependent on the polish. In order to maintain the excellence of the Kiriko, the polish in the final process is important as it determines the attractiveness of the Kiriko.

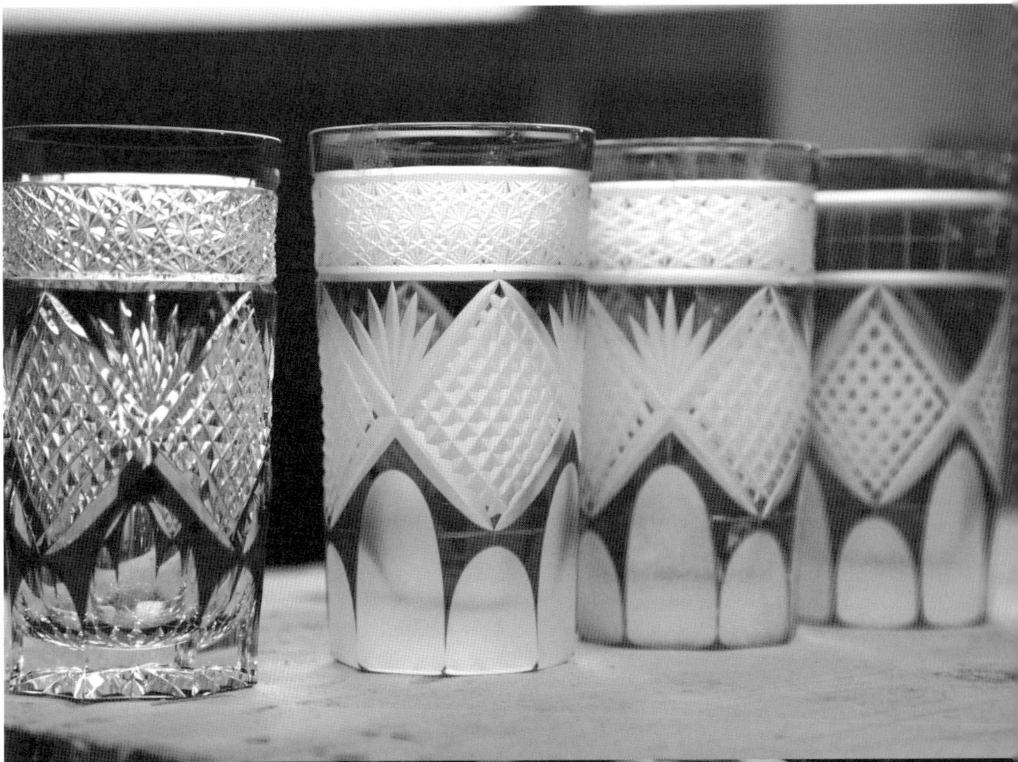

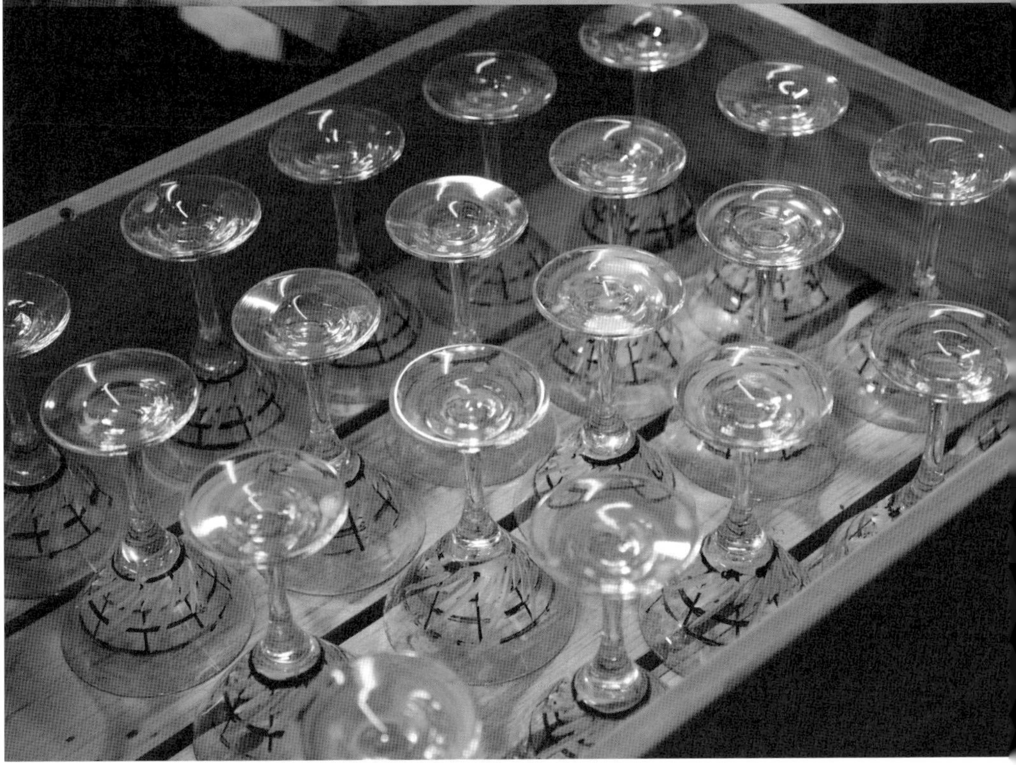

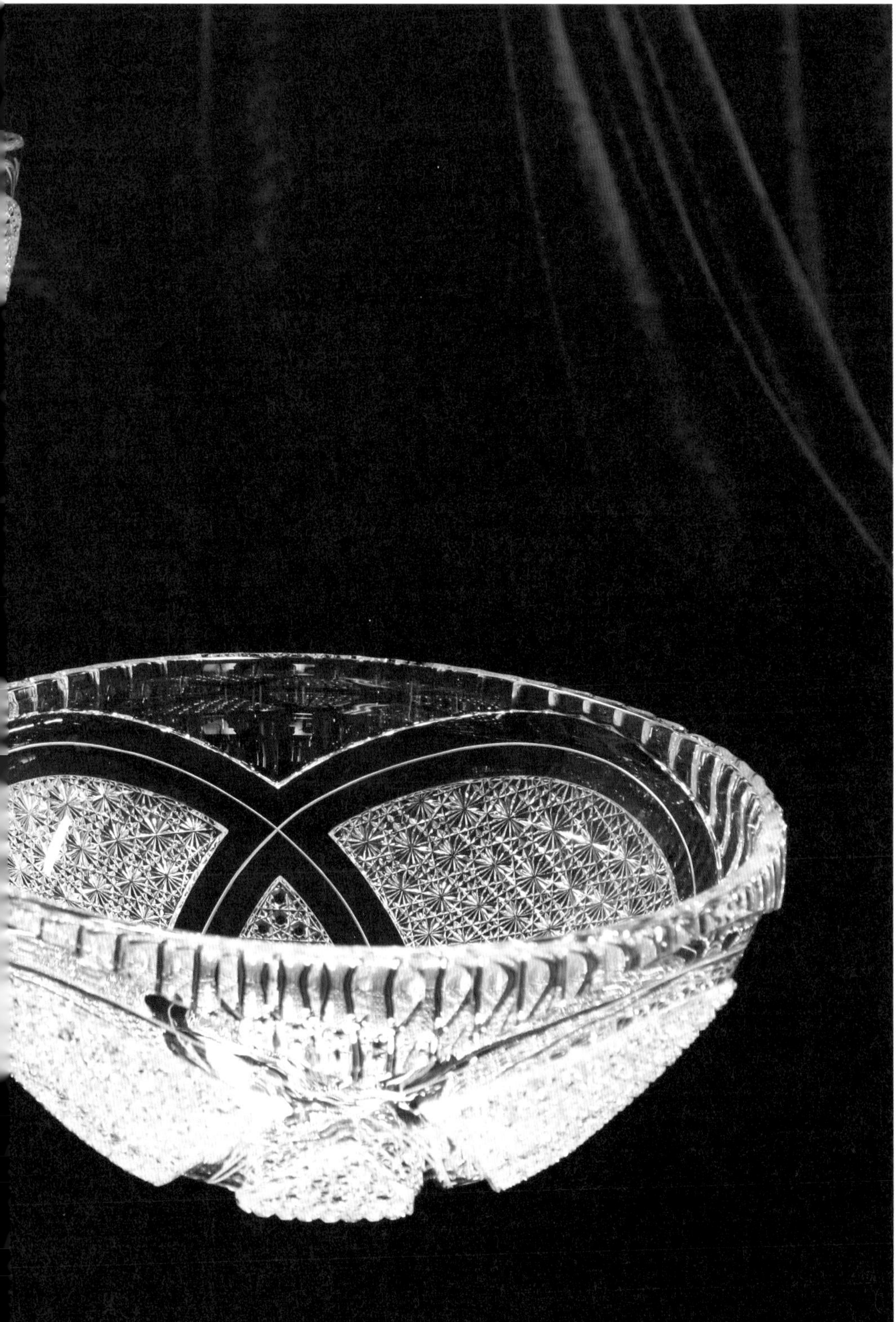

高野秀徳氏・作品

Work of Hidenori Takano

高野秀德先生・作品

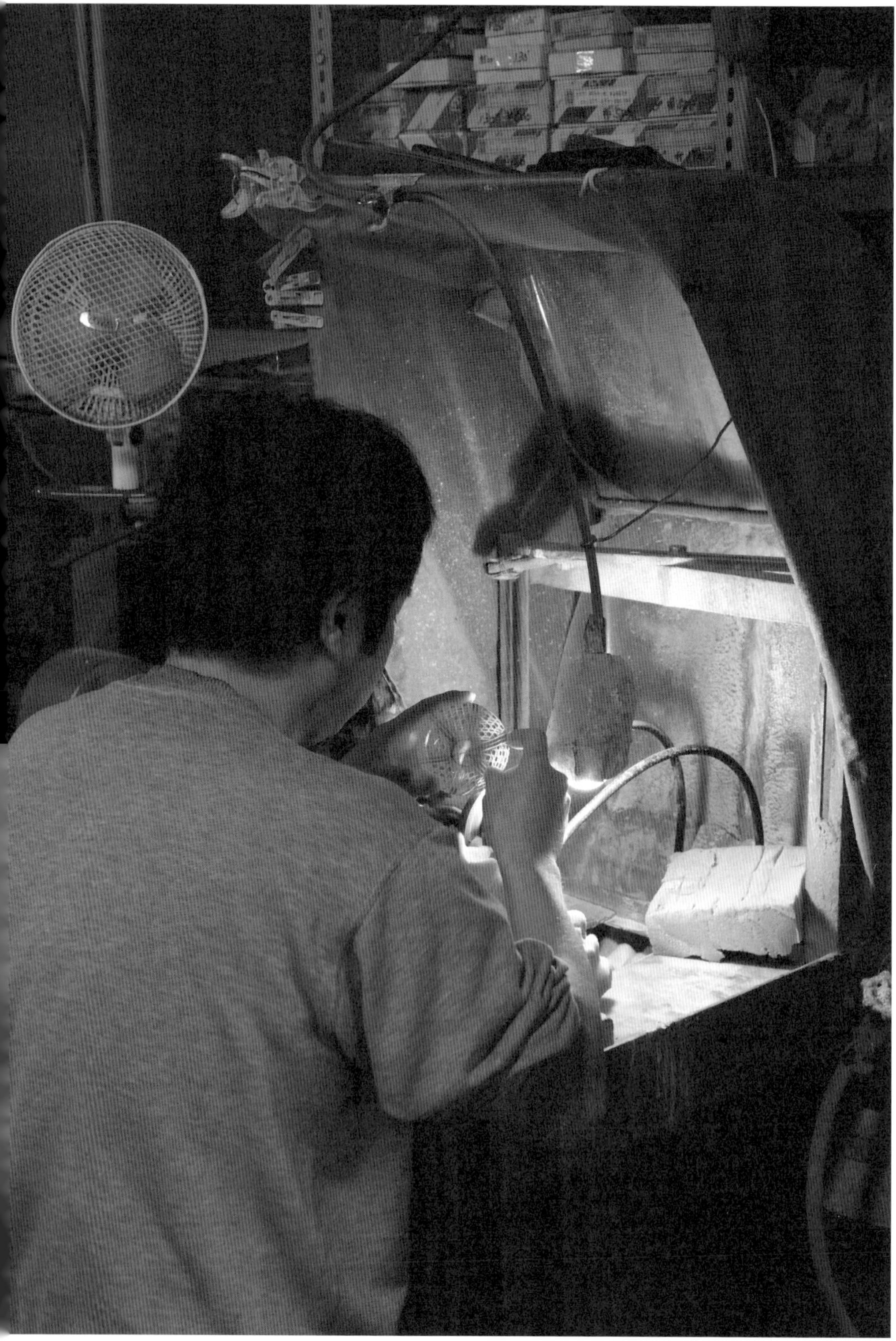

弟子入り、独立

Apprenticeship and Independence

拜師入門、獨立開業

高野秀徳さん

Hidenori Takano
高野秀德先生

いまでは少なくなった、"弟子入り"という修行の仕方。高野さんは子どもの頃から好きだったガラスの世界へ、この"弟子入り"という方法で飛び込み、独立を果たした江戸切子職人。潔くシャープなデザインで数々の賞を手にする、将来を嘱望される若手江戸切子職人は、どのような思いで道を志し、そして独立を果たしたのか。いまも親方の工房の一画で作品を生み続ける、高野さんを訪ね、お話しをうかがってきました。

Nowadays, those taking up the method of learning that is called 'apprenticeships' have become fewer and fewer. Mr. Takano entered the world of glass which he had loved since he was a child by leaping into this method of apprenticeship. He has now achieved his independence and is an Edo Kiriko craftsman. Mr. Takano is a man who has won numerous prizes for his bravely sharp designs. He is a young Edo Kiriko craftsman with a promising future ahead of him. What kind of experiences led him to set his eyes on this path and then his independence? Nowadays, Mr. Takano continues to produce works in one area of the workshop of his master and that is where we visited him to listen to his story.

「拜師入門」這樣的入行方式現在愈來愈少見了。高野先生以「拜師入門」的方式，進入從小就喜歡的玻璃世界，現在已獨立開業成為名副其實的江戶雕花玻璃工匠。高野先生以明晰的設計質感榮獲了多種獎項，被公認為江戶雕花玻璃業界的新希望，他是抱持著什麼心境進入這行的，後來又是怎樣得以成功獨立開業的呢？他至今仍在師傅的工作室的一角繼續創作，現在就讓我們來採訪高野先生，聽他娓娓道來吧。

プロフィール／1968年東京生まれ。伝統工芸士瀧澤利夫氏に師事。1996年高野硝子工芸を開業。第44回、45回伝統工芸新作展入選。第20回伝統工芸諸工芸部会展入選。第23回江戸切子新作展にて「波浪」が経済産業省製造産業局長受賞。2014年経済産業大臣指定伝統的工芸品「江戸切子」伝統工芸士に認定。

個人簡介／1968年出生於東京。向傳統工藝士瀧澤利夫先生學藝。1996年創設高野玻璃工藝。入選第44屆、45屆傳統工藝新作展。入選20屆傳統工藝諸工藝部會展。「波浪」在第23屆江戶雕花玻璃新作展中，榮獲經濟產業省製造產業局長獎。2014年，被認定為經濟產業大臣指定傳統工藝品「江戶雕花玻璃」傳統工藝士。

Profile: Born in Tokyo in 1968. Mr. Takano studied under Toshio Takizawa, a traditional craftsman. In 1996, he opened Takano Glass Crafts. He won prizes in the 44th and 45th Traditional Crafts New Works Exhibitions. He won a prize at the 20th Traditional Crafts, Various Industrial Arts Exhibition. His Ocean Waves at the 23rd Edo Kiriko New Works Exhibition was awarded a prize by the Manufacturing Industry Chief of the Ministry of Economics, Trade and Industry. He was certified as a traditional craftsman of Edo Kiriko Glass which is a traditional art designated by the Minister of Economy, Trade and Industry in 2014.

発注の図面を見ながらチェックする高野さん。

Mr. Takano looks and checks the drawing of an order.

高野先生正在檢視下單圖面。

一度は違う道に。でも、やっぱりガラスが好きだった

「子どものころ、親戚の伯母さんにお小遣いをもらって『好きなものを買ってきていいよ』と言われたことがありました。で、その時に買ったのが小さなガラスのコップ。みんなはお菓子かおもちゃを買ってくると思っていたらしく、意外そうな顔をしていました。そのコップは今でも持っています」と語るのは高野硝子工芸の高野秀徳さん。

中学生の頃は美術や技術が好きで、家が電気設備関連の仕事をしていたこともあり、高等専門学校に進学。そこで電気関係の技術を学び、卒業後は半導体関連の会社に就職しました。「実は就職したものの、すぐに退職。家業の手伝いをしながら、ずっと『一生の仕事は何か』ということを考えていました」という高野さん。知り合いに、前のページで登場していただいた小林淑郎さんのお父様である小林英夫さんを紹介してもらい、小林さんを通じて瀧澤硝子工芸に〝入門〟。

「ガラスについては好きでしたが全く知識も経験もありませんでした。わからない所やうまくいかないとこでも修行は苦になりませんでしたね。

54

ろは親方やほかの人のやり方、作品を見て参考にしました」という高野さん。次第に、依頼された仕事だけでなく、いろいろなことに挑戦したくなり、仕事の時間外に自分の作品制作にも取り組むようにもなったそうです。

「もともと切子は形ができあがった器に模様を刻んでいくワザですが、自分の作りたいものを追求していくと、その形を作るところから勉強したくなりました。ですから、知り合いの吹き硝子の職人さんのところへ行ったり、平面を研磨する『平物』の職人さんのところへ行ったり。同じ切子をやっている、他の職人さんのところへ行くこともありました。私の師匠は懐が深い人で、自由に行き来させてくれたことにはとても感謝しています」という高野さん。

瀧澤硝子工芸に入社して六年目には、晴れて独立。現在は『枠借り』という切子の職人さんならではの方式で、瀧澤硝子工芸の一画を借り、自分の名前で仕事をしています。

「同じ頃に始めて、途中で辞めてしまった人も何人か見ました。やはり、これを一生の仕事にすると決めたら、かじりついてでもやるのだ、という姿勢が大切。親方を始めお世話になった人に恩返しができるようになるのが一人前になることだと思います」。

独立に際しては親方から、『退職金がわりに』ということで機材を譲り受けたという高野さん。「かつて学んだ電気の知識を活かしてチューンナップして使っています」と笑って語ってくれました。

55

切子は周りを比較的暗くし、加工している先端の部分だけを
強い光で照らす方が作業しやすいそうです。

Kiriko has relatively darker carving and so it is easiest to work toward the illumination created by the strong light on just the end of the part that is being processed.

製作雕花玻璃時，四周的燈光會比較暗，只在需要加工的前端部分打上強光，
據說這樣比較便於作業。

Knowing what angle to put the glass into the diamond wheel and how much strength to use demands the technique of an experienced craftsman

在使用鑽石砂輪時,要怎樣調整玻璃的角度,要怎樣施力,這些都需要熟練的技巧。

ダイヤモンドホイールに対して、どのような角度でガラスを当てていくか、どのくらい力を込めるかに、熟練のワザが要求されます。

I once went a different way, But of course, it was glass that I truly loved.

"When I was a child, I received an allowance from my aunt and she told me 'Buy something you like with it.'" At that time the thing I bought was a small glass tumbler. It seemed that everyone expected me to buy some candy or a toy and so they had a surprised look on their faces when they found out what I had done with the money. Even today I still have that tumbler." These are the words of Hidenori Takano of Takano Glass Crafts.

When he was a junior high school student he liked arts and crafts. His family also had jobs related to electrical equipment and so he entered into technical college. At college he learned about electrical technology and after graduation he found employment in a company related to semiconductors. "In fact, although I had found a job, I soon quit. While helping my father with his job I was continuously thinking about 'What kind of job should I spend the rest of my life doing?'" said Mr. Takano. An acquaintance of his introduced him to Hideo Kobayashi, the father of Yoshiro Kobayashi who we had the pleasure of meeting already in this book. Through Mr. Kobayashi he joined Takizawa Glass Crafts. "Although I had liked glass, I had absolutely no knowledge or experience of it at that time." However, learning was not a problem for me. I looked at the pieces and methods of my master and others and I used this as a reference for the things that I didn't understand or the things that I was not good at" mentioned Mr. Takano. Gradually, he developed a desire to tackle not just the jobs that he had been given, but various other tasks as well, and so he started taking on the challenge of producing his own pieces outside of the hours of his job.

"Originally, Kiriko was the technique of engraving a pattern on a vessel whose shape had already been completed. However, when I went in pursuit of making my own pieces, I wanted to learn from the point where these shapes were made. Therefore, I would go to the place of an acquaintance who was a glassblowing craftsman and I would go to see a flat work craftsman who grinds things level. I would also go to meet other craftsmen who were making the same kind of Kiriko. My master is a very broadminded person and so he would let me come and go as I pleased. I am very grateful to him for that," says Mr. Takano.

In his sixth year after joining Takizawa Glass Crafts, he publically went independent. Currently, he is following the unique system of Kiriko craftsmen called wakukari (space borrowing), whereby he is borrowing one area of Takizawa Glass Crafts and working there in his own name.

"I have seen that some people who started in this industry at the same time as me have already quit. It is definitely important to take the attitude that once you have chosen to do this job for life then you should stick to it no matter what. I think that being able to become someone that can repay the kindness that my master showed to me when I was starting out is what will make me come of age."

Upon gaining his independence he was able to use the comparatively generous severance payment from his master to inherit the equipment he uses. "I am able to make use of my knowledge of electricity that I had learned in my previous career to tune up the equipment" spoke Mr. Takano while laughing.

曾經一度從事別的行業，但還是最鍾情於玻璃藝術。

高野硝子工藝的高野秀德先生說：「小時候，伯母曾給我零用錢，她說：『你可以去買自己喜歡的東西。』當時，我買的是一個小玻璃杯。好像大家都認為我會拿錢去買糖果或玩具，所以看到玻璃杯時，他們的臉上都是一副難以置信的表情。至今，我仍然保存著那個玻璃杯。」

高野先生在中學時非常熱衷於美術和技術，因家中從事電器設備相關的行業，於是便選擇就讀高等專科學校，學習電子相關的技術，畢業後進入了半導體公司服務。他說：「其實，我進公司不久後就離職了。離職後，除了幫忙家族事業外，我同時也一直在思考：『什麼是終身職業？』這個問題。」後來，透過朋友介紹，認識了前幾頁介紹的小林淑郎先生的父親—小林英夫先生，並且在小林先生的引薦之下，進入「瀧澤硝子工藝」拜師學藝。

高野先生表示：「我以前很喜歡玻璃，卻完全沒有任何相關知識和經驗。不過，學習的過程卻不引以為苦。遇到不懂的地方或困難時，我會觀摩師傅或別人的做法和作品以做參考。」後來，除了份內的工作外，高野先生也逐漸開始想要進行其他各種挑戰與嘗試。於是，他便利用工作之餘，開始著手創作屬於自己的作品。

高野先生繼續說道：「雕花玻璃本是屬於一種在成形的器皿上刻劃出各式美麗圖樣的技藝，然而一旦追求自己想要的作品時，就會想要從器皿的造型部分開始學習。因此，我開始到處見習觀摩，向認識的吹玻璃工匠和平面研磨工匠請益，偶爾也會拜訪同業的其他工匠切磋技藝。我的恩師是個虛懷若谷的人，我非常感謝他讓我自由遊走在各家之間學習。」

進入「瀧澤硝子工藝」後的第六年，高野先生開始獨立開業。目前，他以業界獨有的『借框』方式，租用「瀧澤硝子工藝」工作室內的一角，以自己的名義進行工作。

「我看過好幾位同時間開始學藝的人半途而廢。畢竟一旦決定以此為終身事業的話，就要有咬緊牙關的決心，這種心態是非常重要的。未來能夠回報恩師及其他前輩時，就表示你已經能夠獨當一面了。」

高野先生提到，獨立開業之際，師傅以『退休金』的名義將機材轉讓給他。他笑著說：「我運用過去所學的電子知識，將機器稍微調整後就可使用了。」

江戸切子への思いを語る高野さん。

Mr. Takano talking about his experiences of Edo Kiriko.
高野先生正在講述自己對江戶雕花玻璃的想法。

連絡先／「高野硝子工芸」　住所／東京都江東区北砂 4-27-8
電話／ 090-5313-0773　※直販は取り扱っておりません

Contact information: Takano Glass Crafts.　Address: 4-27-8 Kitasuna, Kouto-ku, Tokyo
Telephone: 090-5313-0773　* Direct sales are not handled on this number.

聯絡處／「高野玻璃工藝」　地址／東京都江東區北砂 4-27-8
電話／ 090-5313-0773　※恕不接受現場直接銷售

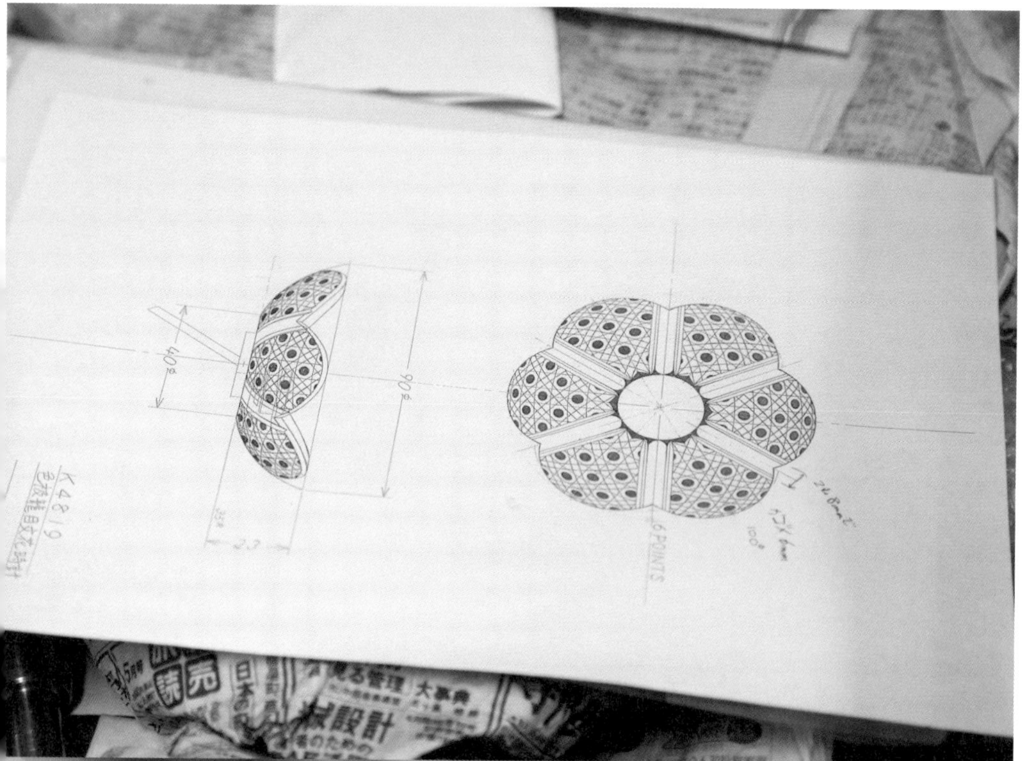

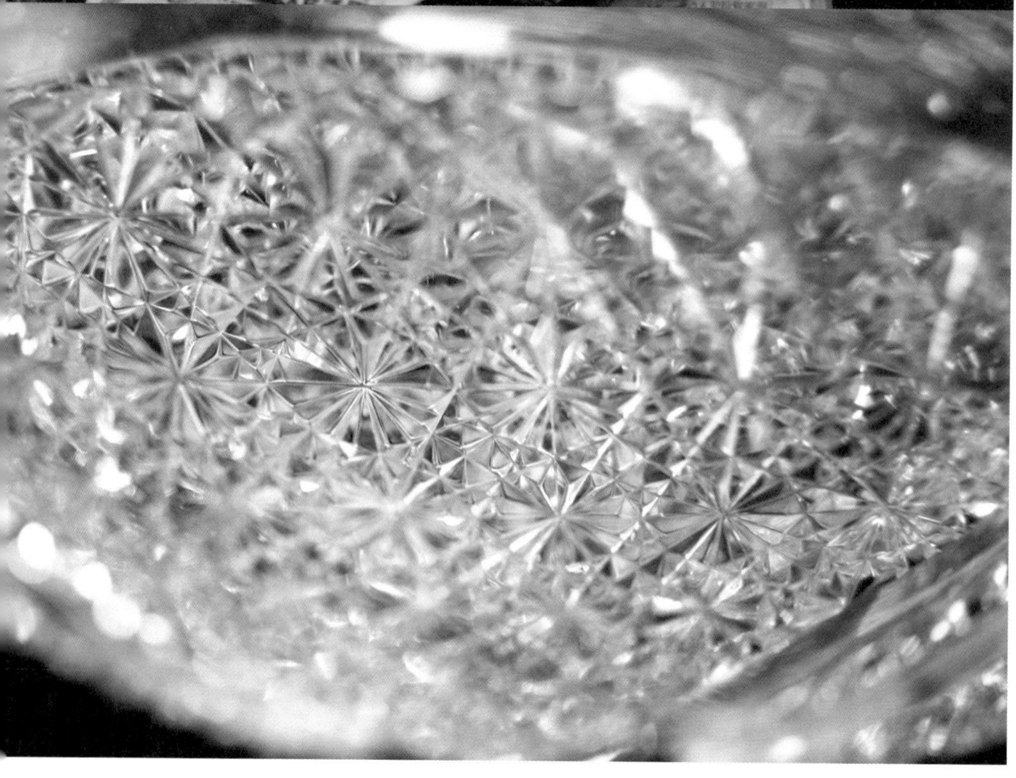

江戸切子の文様

Designs of Edo Kiriko

江戸雕花玻璃的紋飾

美しく繊細に表現した、江戸の人々が愛した多彩な和の文様

江戸切子の典型的な文様のひとつに、細やかなカットによる光の反射が魚の鱗(うろこ)のようにも見える魚子(ななこ)があります。この文様は、イギリスやアイルランドで18世紀から19世紀にかけての典型的なカット文様でもあります。他にも、菊籠目(きくかごめ)・七宝(しっぽう)・麻の葉・矢来(やらい)などの文様があり、さらにそれらを組み合わせるなどした文様が用いられています。これらは、江戸時代から受け継がれてきた、和の繊細な感性を存分に表現したものと言えるでしょう。

江戸の人々にも愛された文様を纏(まと)い、キラリと輝くカットグラスは、思わず手に取りたくなる美しさを放ち、心を惹きつけます。目を凝らしてよく見てみれば、一本一本の線と線の間隔がたいへん狭く、職人の巧みなワザを感じられます。

柔美纖細的手法呈現出江戶人喜愛的多彩和風紋飾

江戶雕花玻璃的典型紋飾之一,即為魚子紋,玻璃器皿表面細膩的雕花,透過光線折射,宛如栩栩如生的魚鱗。這種紋飾同時也是18~19世紀英國和愛爾蘭的代表性雕刻圖樣。其他,另有菊籠目、七寶、麻葉和籠笆等雕花圖案,亦可組合各種不同的紋飾圖形加以運用。以上代表性的花樣,承襲江戶時代裝飾藝術的精神,可說是充分展現出了和風的細膩和感性。

玻璃器皿上雕飾著深受江戶人喜愛的樣紋,閃爍著絢麗多彩的光輝,綻放著令人愛不釋手的美麗風采,憑添無窮的魅力。凝神注視,線形交錯的紋路極為細緻,讓人不得不讚嘆匠師的鬼斧神工。

Delicately beautiful expressions,
The diverse Japanese-style designs that were loved by the people of Edo

In the reflection of light in one representative design of Edo Kiriko, it is possible to see *Nanako* which also looks like the scales of a fish. This was also a representative cut glass design in England and Ireland from the 18th to 19th centuries. Besides this, there are other designs such as the chrysanthemum woven-bamboo pattern, seven treasures, leaf of hemp and fence of bamboo. Furthermore, these designs have been used in various combinations. These designs, which have been handed down since the Edo period, can surely be called expressions that freely show the Japanese-style delicate sense.

This cut glass radiates with a momentary flash of light, wearing these designs that were also loved by the people of the Edo period. They give off beauty such that instinctively you take them in hand and which fascinates your heart and soul. If you try really staring at these designs, you will see that each line and the spaces between these lines are extremely tiny and you will be left with a feeling of the ingenious skill of the craftsmen that made them.

芯無し蜘蛛の巣紋
The spider web with no center crest
無芯蜘蛛的巣紋

魚子
Nanako
魚子紋

菊繋ぎ紋　Chrysanthemum patch crest
菊繋紋

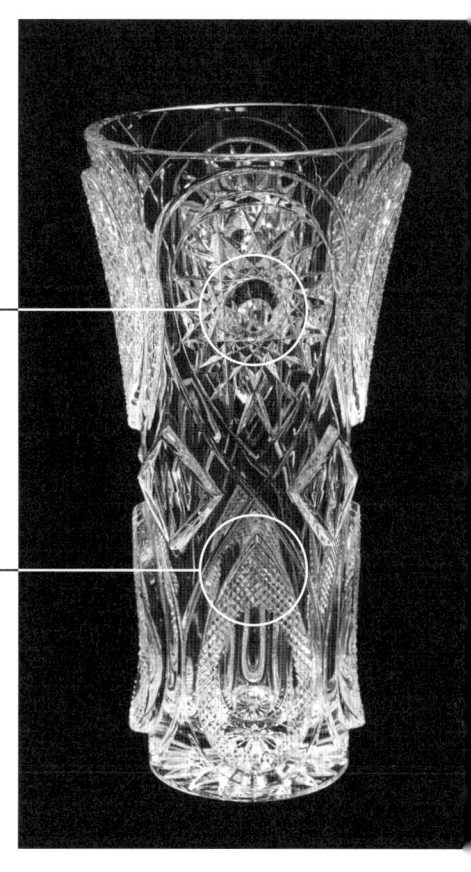

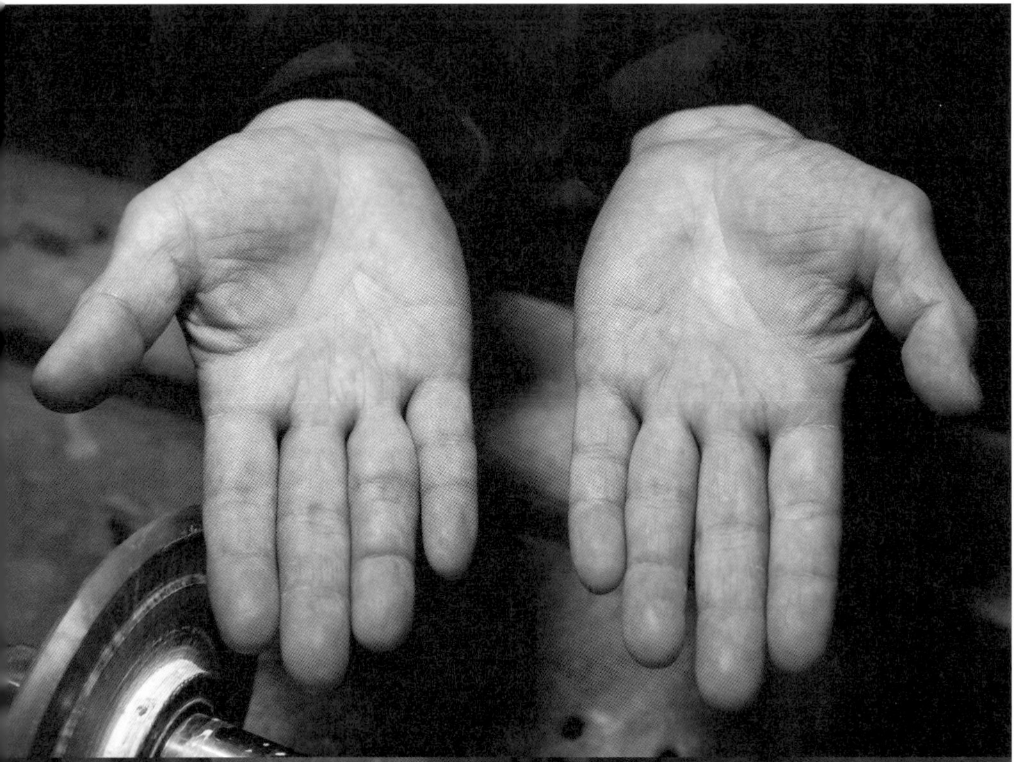
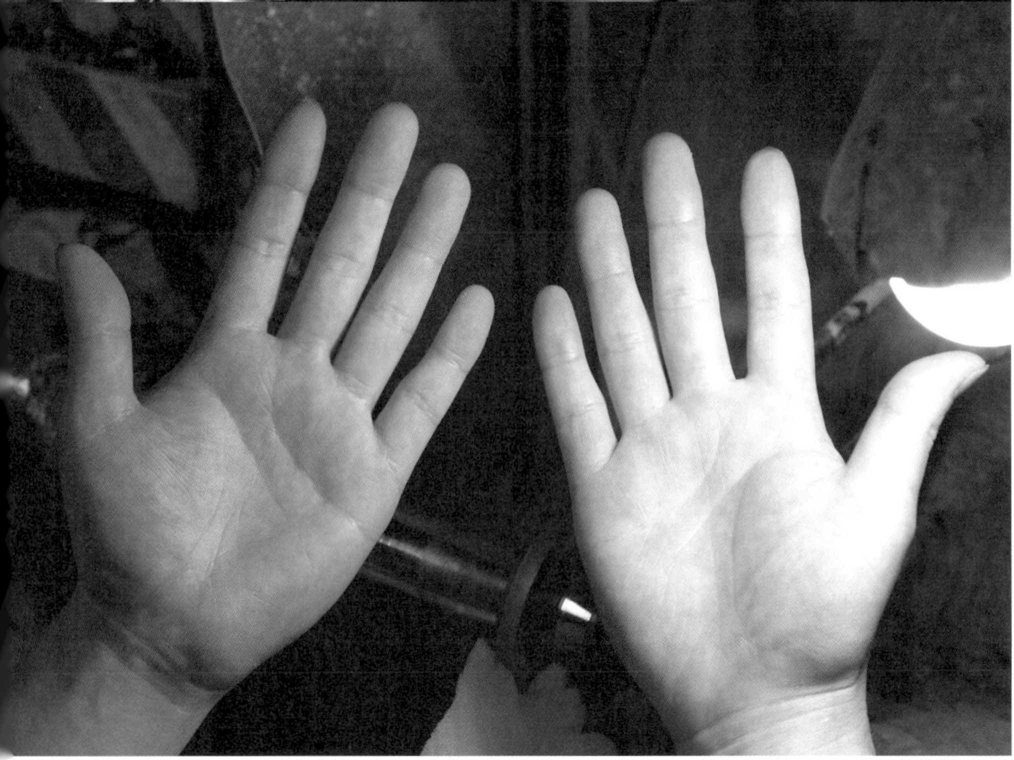

切子職人への道

The Path to Becoming a Kiriko Craftsman

成為雕花玻璃工匠的路程

美しい模様を生み出す器用さと美的感覚が必要

切子職人になるには、切子の特徴である美しい模様をつくり出す、手先の器用さと経験が必要。多くの経験で培った確かな技術と勘が作品の仕上がりを左右します。

また、飾るだけの切子ではなく、グラスなどは毎日の食卓で楽しんでもらえるように、実用性を考えたデザインも大事です。一方、華やかな切子のイメージに反して、作業は一日中椅子に座って行われるので、集中力も不可欠。技術を身につけるためには同じ作業を繰り返し、常によりよいものを目指して挑戦し続けていくことが大事です。

また切子職人にはデザインセンスも重要。ワザの追求には地道に取り組む一方、遊び心も大切。さまざまなものから学んでいく姿勢が必要です。

切子職人に弟子入り。切子工房での見学や体験がお薦め

切子職人になるには、特に資格は必要なく、職人に弟子入りするのが一般的です。学校を卒業後弟子入りする人も多いですが、サラリーマン

須具備巧手與美感品味,
這樣才能創作出美麗的圖樣

想要成為雕花玻璃工匠,必須具備靈巧的雙手與豐富的經驗,才能將雕花玻璃的美感完整呈現。豐富的經驗所累積出來的深厚技術與直覺,將左右作品的整體質感。

還有,雕花玻璃並非只有裝飾的功能,這類的玻璃皿能讓每天的用餐時光充滿樂趣,所以,設計上也不能忽略實用性。另一方面,雕花玻璃雖然給人華麗的印象,但製作雕花玻璃時,卻必須整天坐在椅子上,所以,集中力是絕對不可或缺的。想要習得一身好技術,就必須重複相同的動作,也要經常提升自己的目標,持續接受新挑戰。

另外,製作雕花玻璃的工匠也必須具備設計品味。除了要致力於追求更高的技巧外,玩心創意也不可少。對於各種事物都必須抱持學習的態度,藉以從中獲得設計靈感。

Creating beautiful patterns,
Skillfulness and an aesthetic sense are essential

To become a Kiriko craftsman it is important to have skillful fingers and experience that can create beautiful patterns that are characteristic of Kiriko. The certain techniques and intuition that are cultivated from a great deal of experience determines the finish of the work.

Furthermore, it is also important to be able to create designs that are not just for Kiriko which will be used only as ornaments, but also designs for glass that take into account practical aspects and which can be enjoyed at the dining table every day. On the other hand, in contrast to the glamorous image of Kiriko, because work is carried out by spending all day sitting down, it is essential to have strong powers of concentration. In order to acquire the techniques of Kiriko, the same task must be performed over and over again and it is important to constantly challenge yourself to make better and better pieces.

Moreover, it is vital that Kiriko craftsmen have a sense of design. In the pursuit of these techniques, while it is important to work steadily, it is also essential to have a playful spirit. It is necessary to have an attitude that you are willing to continue learning from a variety of sources in the future as well.

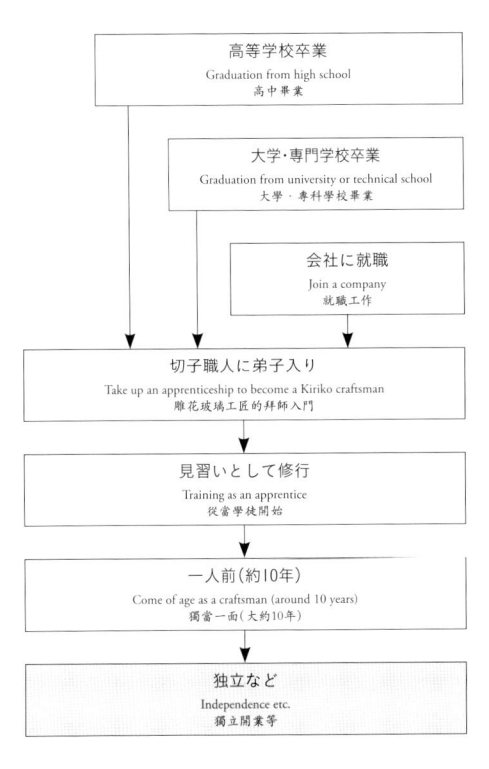

```
高等学校卒業
Graduation from high school
高中畢業
   │
   ▼
大学・専門学校卒業
Graduation from university or technical school
大學・專科學校畢業
   │
   ▼
会社に就職
Join a company
就職工作
   │
   ▼
切子職人に弟子入り
Take up an apprenticeship to become a Kiriko craftsman
雕花玻璃工匠的拜師入門
   │
   ▼
見習いとして修行
Training as an apprentice
從當學徒開始
   │
   ▼
一人前(約10年)
Come of age as a craftsman (around 10 years)
獨當一面(大約10年)
   │
   ▼
独立など
Independence etc.
獨立開業等
```

から転職する人もいます。

切子職人を目指す人には、江戸切子であれば東京都東部地域、薩摩切子であれば鹿児島にある切子工房での見学や体験をお薦めします。

また、本を読むなどして切子に詳しくなるのもいいですが、カルチャースクールなどで切子を学べるので、実際に体感してみるのもいいでしょう。近年、切子の美しさに魅了された女性の職人も増えてきています。

雕花玻璃工匠要拜師入門。建議參觀雕花玻璃工作室並親身體驗。

想成為製作雕花玻璃的工匠，並不需要特別的證照，一般都是以拜師入門的方式開始學藝。有很多人從學校畢業後直接拜師入門，也有些人是從上班族轉行入門的。

有志成為雕花玻璃工匠的人，若想學江戶雕花玻璃的話，建議到東京東部地區，若想學薩摩雕花玻璃的話，則建議到鹿兒島的雕花玻璃工作室去好好觀摩體驗。

還有，透過閱讀自學等方式來了解雕花玻璃，雖然也不失為一個好方法，但因為最近在文化中心等地方，也都能學習到雕花玻璃的相關課程，有機會實際去體驗一下應該也不錯。近年來，有意來愈多女性被雕花玻璃的美所吸引，因而成為雕花玻璃工匠的。

Take up an apprenticeship to become a Kiriko craftsman,
Study and experience at a Kiriko workshop is the recommend path

In order to become a Kiriko craftsman, no special qualifications are required and instead people generally choose to take up an apprenticeship to become a craftsman. Many apprentices come to the profession after graduating from school, but there are also those that are changing their jobs mid-career. For example they might have been an office worker in their previous career.

Those that desire to become a Kiriko craftsman are encouraged to see and experience for themselves a Kiriko workshop. If they wish to learn Edo Kiriko they should go to a workshop in the eastern area of Tokyo. If they wish to learn Satsuma Kiriko they should go to a workshop in Kagoshima.

Moreover, although it is a good idea to read up on Kiriko to learn the finer details, recently it has become possible to learn about Kiriko at culture schools and the like and so surely this would be a great way to actually experience what Kiriko is all about. In recent years, there have also been a growing number of female craftsmen that have been fascinated by the beauty of Kiriko.

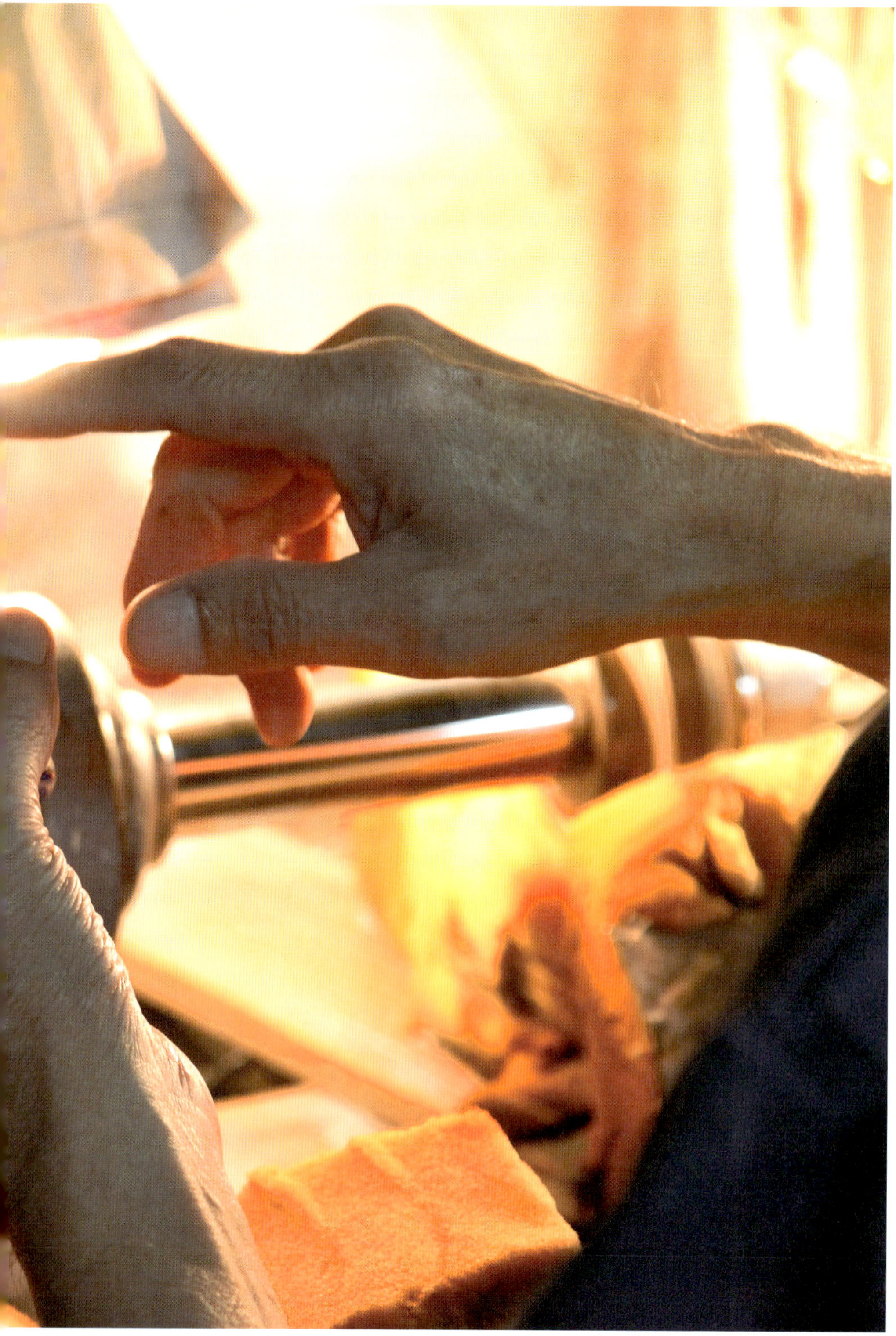

見るなら　If You Want to See　觀摩

江戸時代のガラス製品を常設展示
神戸市立博物館

兵庫県神戸市中央区京町24　電話／078-391-0455
営業時間／10:00〜17:00（入館は16:30まで）ただし金曜日は19:00まで（入館は18:30まで）
休日／月曜（祝日の場合は翌日）、年末年始、その他臨時休館日あり
HP／http://www.city.kobe.lg.jp/culture/culture/institution/museum/main.html

Permanent exhibition of Edo period glass products
Kobe City Museum

24 Kyo-machi, Chuo-ku, Kobe　Telephone: 078-391-0455
Opening hours: 10:00-17:00 (last admission 16:30) However, on Friday's the museum is open to 19:00 (last admission 18:30)　Closed days: Mondays (If this is a public holiday, then the next day will be a closed day), the New Year's holidays and other special closed days
Website: http://www.city.kobe.lg.jp/culture/culture/institution/museum/main.html

平常展示江戸時代的玻璃藝品
神戸市立博物館

兵庫縣神戸市中央區京町24　電話／078-391-0455
營業時間／10:00〜17:00（入館時間到16:30為止）但星期五到19:00為止（入館時間到18:30為止）　公休日／星期一（逢國定假日則為次日）、新年假期、另有其他臨時休館日
Website: http://www.city.kobe.lg.jp/culture/culture/institution/museum/main.html

国内外の代表的名品を所蔵
サントリー美術館

東京都港区赤坂9-7-4 東京ミッドタウン ガレリア3階　電話／03-3479-8600
営業時間／10:00〜20:00（日・月・祝日は18時まで。入館は閉館30分前まで）
休日／火曜、元日、展示替期間（火曜が祝日の場合は開館とし、翌日休館）
HP／https://www.suntory.co.jp/sma/

A collection of domestic and international representative masterpieces
Suntory Museum of Art

Tokyo Midtown Galleria 3F, 9-7-4 Akasaka, Minato-ku, Tokyo
Telephone: 03-3479-8600
Opening hours: 10:00-20:00 (Sundays, Mondays and public holidays closes at 18:00. Last admission is 30 minutes before close)
Closed days: Tuesdays, New Year's Day, exhibit changeover period (If a public holiday falls on a Tuesday then the museum opens and the next day is closed)
Website: https://www.suntory.co.jp/sma/

收藏國內外具有代表性的名品
三得利美術館

東京都港區赤坂9-7-4 東京中城GALLERIA 3樓
電話／03-3479-8600
營業時間／10:00〜20:00（星期日・星期一・國定假日到18時為止。限於閉館前30分鐘入館）
公休日／星期二、元旦、展示品更換期間（星期二若逢國定假日則開館，次日休館）
Website: https://www.suntory.co.jp/sma/

買うなら　If You Want to Buy　選購

江戸切子協同組合のショールーム
江戸切子ショールーム

東京都江東区亀戸4-18-8 亀戸梅屋敷内　電話／03-3684-6321
営業時間／10:00〜17:00　休日／月曜（祝日営業・翌日休）
HP／https://www.edokiriko.or.jp/

Edo Kiriko Cooperation Association Showroom
Edo Kiriko Showroom

Kameido Umeyashiki, 4-18-8 Kameido, Koutou-ku, Tokyo
Telephone: 03-3684-6321　Opening hours: 10:00-17:00
Closed days: Mondays (open on public holidays and closed the following day)
Website: https://www.edokiriko.or.jp

江戸雕花玻璃工業同業公會的展示廳
江戸雕花玻璃展示廳

東京都江東區龜戸4-18-8 龜戸梅屋敷内　電話／03-3684-6321
營業時間／10:00〜17:00
公休日／星期一（逢例假日則營業・次日延休）
Website: https://www.edokiriko.or.jp

葛飾区内の伝統産業の職人の商品が買えます
葛飾区伝統産業館

東京都葛飾区立石7-3-16　電話／03-5671-8288
営業時間／11:00〜18:00　休日／月曜・火曜、夏季・年末年始、その他臨時休館日あり
HP／https://www.dentosangyokan.com/

You can purchase products of craftsmen of traditional industries in Katsushika-ku
Katsushika-ku Traditional Industrial Craftsman Association

7-3-16 Tateishi, Katsushika-ku, Tokyo
Telephone: 03-5671-8288　Opening hours: 11:00-18:00
Closed days: Mondays, Tuesdays, summer season, New Year's holidays, other special closed days
Website: https://www.dentosangyokan.com

可購買葛飾區內傳統產業工匠的作品
葛飾區傳統產業館

東京都葛飾區立石7-3-16　電話／03-5671-8288
營業時間／11:00〜18:00
公休日／星期一・星期二、夏季・新年假期、另有其他臨時休館日
Website: https://www.dentosangyokan.com

掲載の情報は2019年4月現在のものです。
詳しくは各施設のホームページなどでご確認ください。
The information printed here is current as of April 2019.
For more details please check on the website of each institution.
以上為2019年4月現在刊載資訊。
詳情請上各單位的網站自行確認。

職人という生き方
江戸切子

本書編集スタッフ

構成　　　　　木下のぞみ
取材・文　　　ニッポンのワザドットコム編集部
デザイン・装丁　ブレインカフェ
写真　　　　　富野博則
校正　　　　　ブレインカフェ

職人という生き方

江戸切子

二〇一一年七月　第一刷発行
二〇一九年五月　第二刷発行

編者　　　ニッポンのワザドットコム編集部
　　　　　Ⓒ有限会社ブレインカフェ
発行者　　木下のぞみ
発行所　　有限会社ブレインカフェ
　　　　　東京都中央区日本橋富沢町二丁目五番
　　　　　SUビル二階
　　　　　電話　〇三―五六四三―八〇六八（代表）
　　　　　http://www.braincafe.net

印刷・製本　シナノ書籍印刷株式会社

定価はカバーに表示してあります。
造本には充分注意しておりますが、
万一乱丁・落丁がございましたらお取り替えいたします。
本書の無断複写（コピー）は著作権法上の例外を除き、
著作権の侵害になります。

Printed in Japan　ISBN 978-4-905416-00-5　C0072